CW00434596

LES DAWSON'S
LANCASHIRE

LES DAWSON'S

LANCASHIRE

ILLUSTRATIONS BY

JOHN IRELAND

RETRO CLASSICS

RETRO CLASSICS
is a collection of facsimile reproductions
of popular bestsellers from the 1980s and 1990s

Les Dawson's Lancashire was first published in 1983
by Elm Tree Books/Hamish Hamilton Ltd

Re-issued in 2012 as a Retro Classic
by G2 Entertainment
in association with Lennard Publishing
Windmill Cottage
Mackerye End
Harpenden
Hertfordshire
AL5 5DR

Copyright © Les Dawson 1983

ISBN 978-1-909040-28-1

Produced by Lennard Books
a division of
Lennard Associates Limited

Editor Michael Leitch
Designed by David Pocknell's Company Ltd

Printed and bound by Lightning Source

This book is a facsimile reproduction of the first edition of
Les Dawson's Lancashire which was a bestseller in 1983.
No attempt has been made to alter any of the wording
with the benefit of hindsight, or to update the book in any way.

CONTENTS

FOREWORD

I haven't much to say really, but all writers bung something at the beginning of their current masterpiece, don't they? It gives a book a profound sense of occasion and by the time the thing has ground to an indeterminate conclusion, it's too late to ask for your money back. So, I'll light up another cigarette. Actually, I only smoke between meals; yesterday I had forty-six dinners. In a way, this book is a sort of reflective ramble through a large lump of land of which I am most fond. Within its acres no wild species abound, unless one takes in several Blackpool landladies of my acquaintance, but for sheer diversity it has no equal.

Lancashire is many things to many people. It conjures up, for some, vast smoky grey blocks of heavy industry; a place of drab people living uniform lives with strands of cotton festooning their heads; clogs and shawls and flat vowels. To others, however, Lancashire is a memory of lakes and woods and rolling hills, and the object of this book is to discover a Lancashire that is all things to all people.

As that great Oldham philosopher Sam Cocklebottom once remarked: 'Do unto others before they do it to you.'

PART ONE

A RAMBLE IN ARCADIA

MANCHESTER TO THE COAST

Some years ago, I was sat in a pub in Soho. What I was doing there I'll never know, because I'm not a hard drinker; in fact I find it easy. The pub was rather grimy: there were so many cobwebs behind the bar, it looked as if it had been backcombed. I recall dimly that the landlord of the inn was a tall sardonic man with huge ears that made him look like a wing-nut. Our conversation was the usual desultory beer-infected chat: football and women, vile jokes and women, experiences of tasting various brewery products and women . . .

Suddenly, the innkeeper jabbed me in the eye with a finger the size of a Polish sausage and said: 'I've been in the North you know. I once went to Watford.' There and then I realized that for many Britons the world beyond Watford must be shrouded in secrecy. The thought staggered me, I must confess, but I vowed immediately to put matters right. In no uncertain terms I loftily informed the Soho publican that he was nothing but a Southern barbarian; he countered by calling me a Northern git, and his triangular wife threw me into the street. It was the stuff of which novels are retched into life.

Where Else But Lancashire? When one talks of the North of England, again and again the pivot for discussion is Lancashire. Oh, I admit that Yorkshire does exist, but it's such a job to change your money into Leeds currency, and in any case who in their right mind honestly wants to go to Ripon? I once spent a terrible week one night in Bridlington, and I still shudder at the thought of playing a social club in Sheffield. No, let Yorkshire act as ballast, and thank the Lord for the Pennine Chain.

At the foot of Lancashire lies Cheshire. Cheshire is

rather up-market. It's a well-known fact that in Knutsford the Fire Brigade is ex-directory. In Holmes Chapel they take fish and chips home in briefcases, and if you want red cabbage in Macclesfield you get it through Interflora. There are some nice pubs in Cheshire, but the noses of the barmaids are so high in the air, their nostrils look like sunglasses. At least, though, Cheshire protects Lancashire from the Midlands, and for that we can forgive them anything.

Polyglot Manchester I was born in Manchester in the Thirties. It was a depressed decade and most of the people who lived in

our area *were* decayed. Our terraced house was so narrow, the mice walked about on their back legs and the kitchen ceiling was so low the oven had a foot-level grill. The place I was born in was called Collyhurst; it lay two miles from the city centre and it was a district of narrow streets and tenements that gazed eyeless onto cobbled roads escorting the warehouses and shops past shadowed alleyways where teeming hordes of ill-dressed children ran amok. But it was a place that held warmth and comradeship in adversity, and there was compassion and love among the inhabitants.

There is no city in the world like Manchester. Not only is it the centre of the country's commerce, it is also the home of national newspapers, the Hallé Orchestra, the Manchester Ship Canal and great beers such as Boddingtons, Chester's Bitter, otherwise known as 'Lunatic Broth', Threlfall's Ales and Swales's. Eeh, tha's nowt to touch it.

Manchester is Piccadilly and Market Street and fine hospitals such as the Royal Infirmary and St Mary's, and the noble Christie's Hospital that fights cancer and leads the world in its research. The second largest airport in the realm is Ringway which extends into Cheshire, but, by Timothy! only just. The costume museum in Platt Fields is a sonnet to history and Manchester art galleries make the Louvre look like a junk shop. At one time, Manchester had more night clubs than Las Vegas and I've died in most of them.

Manchester was, and still is, the crucible for all races and creeds: Cheetham Hill, Lower Broughton and Prestwich – there you rub shoulders with polyglot humanity, with Hebrew speakers, Ukrainians and the merchants of the Near East. In the side streets, tailors sit cross-legged and create dreams in cloth, and the sound of the sewing machines plays a descant to the yells of the outdoor traders.

I remember the Whit Walks, the long processions of faith down Oldham Street. Little kids marching proudly in new shoes, the first they had ever known. Catholic and Church of England banners floated behind the massed bands, encouraged on their way by knots of people shouting from pub doorways: 'Ere, there's our Lily' and 'Play up, our Alf, the bloody drum's drowning you out.' Some wags used to suck lemons as the bandsmen went by, and before long mouths would dry and the music would become a wail.

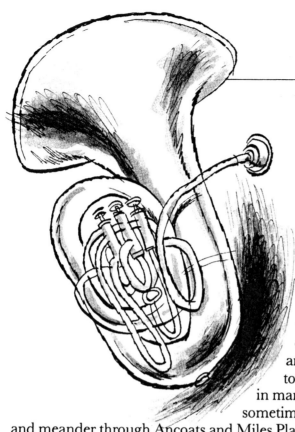

The hit of the Walks was the Italian parade, always colourful and majestic. Manchester has been the home for Italian ice cream makers for ages, and they have contributed to the character of the city in many ways. How I yearn sometimes to turn the clock back and meander through Ancoats and Miles Platting, then on to Moss Side where the black population's culture has blended in with the Irish of Hulme and Greenheys. Despite the ruthless modernization that has tended to destroy the Manchester I knew, the character of its people keeps alive the crowded friendliness that is the hallmark of the city. Some good things have emerged. The River Irwell is cleaner than it has ever been. I remember it used to be so polluted that the fish living in it didn't have fins, they had grease nipples.

'What Manchester does today, London does tomorrow.' That was the proud boast of yesteryear and I think it still applies today. There is an energy about Manchester that seems lacking in other cities, and if you see what the pigeons can do to a statue in Albert Square, the birds have it too.

I did warn you that this book would become a ramble, and in my opinion that is how it should be. After all, when one roams about a country lane, there are so many things to look at and pick up that it is impossible to keep an ordered outlook. In thinking about Lancashire, I remember the words of Harcourt Ramsey, the Burnley poet and tripe dresser, who said: 'A boiled owl in cardboard never drops a claw.' Frankly, I haven't a clue what he was talking about, but it remains with me.

Ticket To Valhalla It is time to move on . . . to 1960, the year I was led to the altar dressed in the black garb of the sacrificial male. I have never forgotten my marriage, although they do say that time is a great healer. My wife stood at my side in her regal white splendour, and with her being such a size, I felt as if I was squatting at the foot of an Alp.

   I recall whispering to the vicar: 'Sanctuary,' but he did not heed my plea and the ceremony went along with yours truly trembling in the manner of a tethered goat waiting for the puma to leap. After the wedding and subsequent honeymoon, which became known as 'The Oxbow Incident', my wife and I, although teetering on the rim of penury, put a deposit down on a small bungalow in the Lancashire township of Bury.

   Bury is a typical mill settlement with two outstanding features: an open market and the world-famous Black Pudding. There has never been anything to touch a well boiled, heavily seasoned Black Pudding. As a weapon of defence it can acquit itself with honour and make an opponent reel in a comatose

state; but to digest . . . ah! Steamy, ebon and fatty, it is at its most
noble when swilled down with a pint of Old Peculiar. Also in Bury
they sold a variety of cowheel that was a gourmet's ticket to Valhalla,
and the tripe was a sheet of pure ecstasy. At Bury market, my wife
purchased clogs for our kids . . . marvellous things, clogs. Iron and
leather in composition, no child could ever mutilate them as they can
ordinary footwear, and if you threw a brat in the canal, he stayed
under.

We lived in a district known as Unsworth. Legend
has it that Henry the Eighth rode to hounds there, and was oft heard
to prate: 'By gum, it's worth the 'uns to come here.' He never
travelled by British Rail, that's for sure; even in 1960 the service was
so slow, if a man tied his wife to the railway track the chances were
she would starve to death.

The posh side of Bury was Walshaw, which nestled
at the foot of moorlands upon which the remains of the Old Roman
Way could clearly be seen with several hunched pubs sheltering from
the roaring winds that swept across that craggy terrain.

A long road led from Bury to Rochdale through an
area called, believe it or not, Jericho. Grand folk they were in Jericho,
with more than a Biblical feel about them. On the corner of one
street there used to sit a strange ragged man with no arms and legs,
and occasionally he would shout: 'I don't want your sympathy or
your money.' Local wags used to say all he wanted was for someone
to scratch his arse.

Ah, Rochdale I always liked Rochdale, there was something about
the place: a warmth and a sort of lovable nosiness that personified
the inhabitants. The town itself was virtually a prisoner of the
towering hills that sat atop in a frowning ring. For sheer Gothic
splendour, Rochdale Town Hall took one's breath away, and a
cleaning woman on the first floor would always look like Gracie
Fields, who was of course Rochdale's very own superstar.

In nearby Milnrow, fish and chip shops abounded,
all of them intelligently situated next to public houses and urinals.
Milnrow struggled on to Littleborough, a place torn apart with a
horror that only Edgar Allan Poe could have devised: half
Littleborough came under the jurisdiction of Yorkshire! But the
hardy Lancastrians took it in their stride and hurled food parcels
across the cobbled lanes.

I might add that I once courted a lass from Rochdale. She was a small girl, in fact she was so small she had wheels fitted on her earrings; but eeh, what a champion she was. Funny though, in some ways; she used to lick my cheek. I said to her once: 'Do you lick my face because you love me?' 'Nay,' she replied through a mouthful of hake. 'I do it 'cos I need the salt.' Actually she came from Castleton which lay on the rim of Rochdale, a smallish place with a canal running through it and, here we go again, some wonderful darkling pubs with interior brass fittings and buxom barmaids with lips like innertubes.

But Where To Begin? Describing Lancashire is like attempting to draw a portrait of a face seen only once – where to begin? The flat plains of East Lancashire? Ormskirk, Southport, Atherton, Leigh, St Helens? Or should we make a start on the Trough of Bowland, Garstang or Kirkby Lonsdale fells? Then there is central Lancashire with Chorley and Blackburn and Padiham jostling for attention. Let's first have a look, a long look, at a sea port that is famous or infamous whichever way you care to view it. Seafaring men all over the world know of this harbour; history records the slave trade there; the mighty liners that ploughed the oceans all berthed there. Yes, it has to be . . .

De Pewel It must be said, I'm afraid, that so-called Modern Development committed murder in Liverpool. It ripped the heart out of a truly noble city leaving gaunt concrete fingers and wastelands to the people of the night, muggers and defrocked VAT men. The humour of Liverpool is the one thing, thank heaven, that can never be demolished, for in the flat harsh Scouse accent lies the beauty of that vast coastal sprawl.

Two years ago, I performed in pantomime in Liverpool, at the venerable Empire on Lime Street, and in the fifteen weeks I was there, every night was an experience. I remember on the opening night, the villain in the show stalked to the footlights and boomed to the audience, most of whom were dock re-settlement kids with shaven heads and pins in their cardigans in place of buttons: 'I am the bad robber and I'll come down amongst you and cut your throats.' A foolhardy line, it seemed to me; sure enough the answer came straight back from the toffee-streaked front-row seats: 'Yer do that, lardy, and we'll kick you in the goolies!' Suffice to say, the villain

retreated in fearful trepidation. The fairy did little
better. In her scant costume she warbled a ditty,
and from a thousand vocal chords issued the
words: 'Gerr 'em off, tarty!'

The average Liverpudlian possesses the uncanny ability of being able to put a string of improbable words together and in so doing produce a verbal painting. For instance, I was talking to a Scouser in an inn off Lime Street, and I asked him if he was still living in The Dingle, which was a slum area of the city. His reply had me in hysterics: 'Naw, we got rehoused in Kirby, it's arlright like but er, de house is small . . . it's really a vampire's haversack.' Now, I ask you . . . a vampire's haversack. That is Liverpool, my friend, and you have to accept it on the terms that it lays down. No pretence whatsoever, and if you try to put on airs and graces, they'll call you a 'gobshite'.

A total stranger getting off the train at Lime Street Station would expect anything except what confronts him. Lime Street Station possesses all the radiant charm that one usually associates with a Murmansk slaughterhouse. The grime of generations has caked the place with layers of fossilized muck and the air one breathes is the same sort that I once inhaled whilst passing a sick elephant. So dirty is the place, the local wags used to say: 'Don't forget to wipe yer feet, la', before yer leave the station.' Once outside the smoky terminal, the aspect changes. Across the wide stretch of Lime Street, an edifice of neo-Grecian splendour shoulders the skyline – St George's Hall. Looming above us mere mortals, its yawning columns are a sonnet to the trade of the architect. However, as one might expect in Liverpool, there is one small point to mull over. St George's was built the wrong way round by its mainly Irish workforce. What should be the front is the back . . . and the man who designed it, shot himself.

On the same street is the regal-looking home of the Liverpool Symphonia. Lime Street then rolls down the very steps of the Adelphi Hotel, the scene of my first cabaret engagement in Liverpool. I won't dwell on that most unhappy of experiences; suffice to say that I died so badly, in India they were calling me the Fourth Prophet. I well recall one beefy gentleman, who reeked of a rot-gut brew, coming over to me and saying: 'Hey der, lardy, can I give yer a word of constructive criticism?' I muttered: 'Of course, sir.' He nodded his head, lit a Woodbine butt and replied: 'I think yer crap.'

Despite my early struggles in Liverpool, I genuinely fell in love with the city. From the seafront with the towers of the great commercial shipping lines leading the turgid Mersey to the ocean and the Liver Bird watching, a silent sentinel, to the dark streets of Chinatown and thence to the awesome bulk of the Anglican Cathedral . . . I came to love it all. I loved the people and the humour that has carried them through so many turbulent epochs:

A comedian in a club: 'I was brought up by a billy goat . . . we couldn't afford a nanny.'

An old lady in a pub of great renown, Ma Egerton's off Lime Street: 'Hello der, son, I've haven't been well . . . I've had everything taken away . . . very serious it is, it's called an hysterical rectumy.'

The bent old man who sold papers near where Paddy's Market used to stand: 'They've pulled our 'ouse down to make way for a sewer.'

The mother of the schoolboy who was sent home because he smelt. The teacher gave the youngster a note for his mother suggesting that she might, perhaps, bathe her offspring. The following day, a hulking lady arrived at the school dragging her urchin behind her. 'Are you the feller wot gave 'im ther note like?' she asked of the teacher. He nodded and was about to explain, when the female grabbed him by the throat and thundered: 'Look 'ere you, 'e's 'ere to read and write – not smell like a bleedin' geranium.'

One year I had a week's booking at an ex-theatre turned night club called the Shakespeare. I didn't finish the week, because on the Thursday they had a fire that reduced the place to a smouldering ruin. I stood outside with the manager as the Fire Brigade lads doused the flames, and I turned and said to him: 'Terrible thing to happen. I never expected this.' He nodded his head and shot back: 'Dead right der, Les. It should have happened Tuesday as first planned.'

Across the Mersey, dear reader, you find New Brighton. Once it was a resort to be reckoned with; now, alas, oil slicks coat the damp sands and the water that laps the shore is so heavily polluted, even an atheist can walk on the water. Once, you could get on board the *Royal Iris* and dance your passage to New

Brighton; the drink flowed like a faulty sluice and the girls left morality behind. But there is a charm about New Brighton and a strong civic pride which is refreshing, and even as this book is being shaped there are plans to turn it back to the time when it knew its finest hour. Of course, the usual route to the resort is via the Mersey Tunnel, that supreme tribute to man's endeavour; indeed, to drive through the tunnel at rush hour is a feat more worthy than a canoe expedition up the Nile.

Out of Liverpool by the northerly route, passing the docks and the slums of Scotland Road – of 'Maggie May' fame – where the pubs and brothels cater for frustrated mariners, we find ourselves in Bootle which, although still a dockland area, has a more dignified look about it.

Hold on, Dawson, we came through Everton on the way, didn't we? In the name of sanity, man, mention the football club. Everton FC. Thank God for that. If I had left them out, some day I might have been found in a sack floating in a culvert. I might have been saved by a Liverpool supporter, but it's best not to count on such things. One thing is certain, though: never discourse on Liverpool without waxing enthusiastic about soccer. To some people, football is merely twenty-two young men propelling a leather sphere across a green sward, with intent to place the said sphere between two upright baulks of timber with a piscatorial-type net hanging from them. To a Liverpudlian it is Life itself, and let no man tear it asunder.

So for now, farewell Liverpool, home of yet another milestone in history – The Beatles. See? There I go again, missing out the pop group that galvanized the world into a new orbit of mass hysteria . . . Wow, what with all the near-omissions so far, the next time I venture into the realm of the Scouse, I'd better take out tar-and-feather insurance. But we digress.

Pleasant Wigan Wigan is one of my favourite towns. It is a pleasant place full of hulking Rugby League players and, despite the music-hall joke about the Pier, a town of great interest. It was in Wigan that I met a man who for me epitomizes the rugged nature of Lancashire. When I met him, I was a cub reporter with a small newspaper, the circulation of which was smaller than the network of veins in a prawn's leg. I sat in the drawing-room of his large home set in thirty acres of deer park, and interviewed him about his fame and his riches, and his beginnings.

'My boy,' he boomed over a glass of gin and tonic. 'I came to Wigan as a callow youth, and all I had in the world was the one suit of clothes I stood up in. I was barefoot with a bundle tied on the end of a stick when I first walked into Wigan.' He paused, puffed heavily on his Cuban cigar, and added with satisfaction: 'That was only ten years ago, and now I own three cinemas, four blocks of real estate, six night clubs and a chain of supermarkets. I have three Rolls Royce saloons and an aeroplane, and a villa in Cannes.'

I sat open-mouthed listening to him. What a success story to give incentive to the restless youngsters of today. I leaned forward in my chair, pencil poised, and I said to him: 'Tell me, sir, what did you have in the bundle on the end of the stick?'

He yawned and replied: 'Fifteen million pounds.'

The Prostrate East East Lancashire is flat. If one sees the slightest hummock, it's either a buried sofa or the work of a mole with gout. Along the coast from Crosby and Formby towards the sedate crouch of Southport, the land is a quiltlike pancake and usually moist. Harcourt Ramsey, the Burnley poet, said of East Lancs: ''Tis an ear-ache in August that ruins thy elbow.' Again, I haven't a clue what he meant but I suppose it kept him off the streets. Market gardeners have their plots here; small stalls sell you carrots the size of a wrestler's thigh, and cows with 'flu muck about in watery troughs.

One old man used to go around shouting: 'Manure, get your manure here – hand-picked!' A local clergyman admonished the old man's wife: 'Why on earth,' said the good man, 'don't you get your husband to shout "Fertilizer"?' The old man's wife wiped her cigar butt on her dungarees and replied: 'It took me ten years to get him to shout "Manure".'

I like to think that story is true.

Let us now, dear reader, ere you nod off in mid-page, stroll down Lord Street in Southport. Long, wide and tree-furbished, Lord Street is a poem to late-Victorian wrought-ironwork. The genteel arcades and shops are freely ornate with metal latticework adorning their walls and fronts, and the effect is one of stability in a changing world.

The main problem with Southport is the sea – or the lack of it. There simply isn't any these days, and locals do say that fish arrive on the shoreline wearing sandals. The earth is being reclaimed from the briny. The pier juts out in lunatic defiance and the riptide couldn't reach it even if you gave it a dose of ginseng. I have seen little children walk out to find the sea, usually with a packed lunch under one arm, and they have returned fully matured and ready for the knackers. There is a marina now where the sea once lapped, and cars park where hulking great halibut used to fornicate. But Southport is very attractive both in its architecture and setting, and not too far away lies the mighty Royal Birkdale golf course.

I have lost more balls at Birkdale than any golfer living today. I have spent so much time in the bunkers on that course, I suffered for years from sand fly fever. It was on the fifth green that my caddy, a dour youth from Hesketh Bank (a small hamlet near Southport that is so far off the beaten track, Dracula got in for the Liberals), delivered the death knell to my game. I asked him if he'd noticed any improvement in me. He snarled and said in a sibilant tone: 'Oh yes, you've had your hair cut.'

I didn't take offence, I merely smacked him with a mashie and dumped his remains out of bounds. Southport boasts, and quite justifiably so, a number of excellent eating-houses that cater for all tastes. Some of them are quite upper-bracket. I took my wife into one of them: it was so high-class, the man on the door gave me a tip. We sat down and the head waiter came over. 'Excuse me, sir,' he spat. 'Have you got a reservation?' I replied somewhat tartly: 'What the hell do you think I am, hey? A bloody Red Indian?' He glanced at the wife and said softly: 'Well, you must be a brave.' Without any preamble, he brought the soup. 'What sort of soup is this?' I asked him. 'It's oxtail, sir,' he responded. 'There's not much of it,' said I, sternly. 'There's hardly enough to cover the bottom.' He peered down his nose and sneered: 'There was on the ox.'

The wife can be most embarrassing on such outings. In Southport there is a delightful Chinese restaurant, and on another occasion I took her there for a small repast. She asked the waiter for chicken. He bowed and said: 'Arsoo.' The wife clenched her formidable jaw and replied icily: 'No, thanks, I'll have a wing.' That's my wife all over. I'm not saying she's ignorant, but if she ever has a brain operation it will cost about fourpence, and that will include search fees.

Southport has a first-class theatre in the shape of the Floral Hall. I know because I played a summer there with that delightful lass Dana, and all the cast enjoyed the amenities that Southport has to offer. There is plenty for the kids there and more advanced things for the teenagers. For well-established drinkers like myself, wonderful pubs lurk in the environs of said resort, and in some of them the old Lancashire Shuttle Dance is still practised when there is a Friday in the week. It's a simple reel and a joy to watch. Two pairs stand in line and shove a ferret up a vicar's kilt, and when he yodels 'Mammy' in Dutch, three of you stand with your back to the traffic and wallpaper each other's legs.

Aye, there's some grand things in Lancashire.

Underneath Oldham In our county we have always had our fair share of eccentrics. Oldham produced Seth Bottlecrud, a tiny man with visible acne who blindfolded himself every time he pulled his socks up. It was he who swore that underneath Oldham lay a vast lake of vindaloo curry. He was a curious chap who owned a lighthouse on the Pennines; he eventually fell into a vat of liquid blackcurrant jelly and now he's set for life.

I used to play the piano in all the inns of Oldham. There was the Regent, the Top Drum, Dr Syntax, the Greaves Arms. The inhabitants of Oldham loved my piano playing, they used to swarm over to the pub where I was performing and break all the windows to hear me better.

But we have digressed again. Let's now leave Oldham and return to the coast.

Before we get there – as so often happens – someone has asked the driver if he can halt awhile in Ormskirk. As I gaze through steamy windows at this delightful market township, I am immediately reminded of that wonderful son of Ormskirk who invented electric braces for people with tall knees. What a boon to mankind that would have been, had they not taken him away to a large house patrolled by bloodhounds. Some people say that he was put away because he embarrassed the Government of the day. From what I could gather, he sold several hundred pairs of his electric braces to an Arab potentate, who in turn supplied them to his army. Apparently, in a pitched battle with marauding Riffs, the cut-out switches on the braces melted with the heat, and his troops found their trousers three feet above their heads. This led to confusion, as one would expect, and ultimate defeat. In retaliation, the potentate shoved ninepence on a gallon of two-star and cancelled his holiday in Rhyl.

The Trouble With Preston Restored at last to our original route, we leave Southport, lofty old doyenne with her airs and graces. The countryside we traverse is still flatter than a postman's feet, and when the wind blows in from the sea, it's so cold they have to lag the brass monkeys.

Within an hour we reach Preston. What can one say about that ignoble pile? The trouble with Preston is that it has no clearly defined shape, but lies like an elderly water buffalo with prostate problems. Of course, Preston used to be a fairly important shipping harbour, dealing with timber boats from Scandinavia, but that is now defunct.

It is in the roots of history that Preston plays its uncompromising role: there the opposing armies of Yorks and Lancs fought bitterly, hurling bread puddings at each other with gusto during the Civil War. Was it not Bonnie Prince Charlie who rode

through the town until a breeze lifted his kilt and froze his sporran?

Not only is the town steeped in history, so is its football team – a team so bad these days, if they get a corner they do a lap of honour. The dark waters of the River Ribble dissect the confused terrain and the whole effect is worthy of Hogarth. Having said which, Preston is a lively place and is also the home of the British Aircraft Corporation which makes aeroplanes that go so fast, you can have breakfast in New York and burp in Moscow. But again, it is the people who make a town, not the soot-grimed bricks, and the townsfolk are typical Lancastrians with very large hearts. They still say 'Excuse me' before they mug you.

Outside Preston, to the south, lies Penwortham, the home of a first-class golf club. Alas, some of the fairways are so high, players are tempted to hit the ball with oxygen cylinders.

Now we head west once more, past the old Playhouse Repertory Company, leaving behind the Polytechnic and the maze of new road systems and high-rise commercial buildings, and speed down the dock road towards the main highway that will lead us gaily to the Fylde. Once we leave behind the platoons of pylons that desecrate the area, suddenly the air grows cleaner and we worm our way into that most sublime of hamlets . . . Freckleton.

ROMANTIC FYLDE

This landmass is worth a chapter on its own. For one thing, I live in the Fylde, and if the council like this book I might get a rates rebate.

We are soon through Freckleton; it's a small place, in fact the speed-limit signs are back to back. Apart from one or two excellent public houses, Freckleton is about as interesting as listening to a lecture on the mating habits of the East Malaysian dung beetle. There are scores of garden nurseries beside the road and they can be worth a browse; personally I haven't got green fingers, although my neck is a funny colour.

A Niche In My Heart We are now in Lytham. Leafy, dreaming Lytham that holds a special niche in my heart. It was in dear Lytham, twenty-two years ago, that the wife's mother was kidnapped. At half-past nine in the morning, the ransom money was two hundred pounds; by half-past eleven it was one and sixpence, and the last I heard, the kidnappers had paid the money in themselves. I cannot blame them, that gorgon is so ugly, when she went to see the film *The Elephant Man,* the audience thought she was making a personal appearance.

The thing that fascinates me about Lytham is that no matter how many times you walk down Clifton Street, you always find a little shop you never saw before. Shops, shops, shops – everywhere you peer, you see tiny cramped shops that beckon you within to sample their delights; antique shops by the bushel; greengrocers, pie shops with aromatic smells that haunt the senses; art shops with near-sighted old ladies to serve you . . . There are tea shops and odd cafés, pottery shops and wool shops; they all jostle one another for the keys to your wallet.

On the sea front is the old Lytham windmill, flanked on all sides by wide swards of greenery. The air is so bracing as it buffets your cheeks, and cajoles out a reddish hue, you will soon feel like a coy maiden hurrying to a tryst. Dally awhile and gaze down Clifton Drive, that broad highway which sweeps before you in

the manner of a haughty duchess. What majesty! There are dinghies and yachts bobbing about in the Lytham waters; hearty men with reefer jackets and pipes talking about the movement of shrimps; young lovers huddling in shelters and making furtive bodily explorations, and dogs doing bowel things on the sands. The pubs (yes, pubs again) are doing a brisk trade with Boddingtons Ales and dark cool Hartley's, and the old ladies sit on benches in Lytham Square and expose Tudor underwear, thus giving rise to the expression 'knicker pavilion'. Lytham is delightful and charming, and any dreaded town planner who yearns to change it should be very carefully minced.

We trot along past Lowther Gardens, scene of many a garden fete, some of which I myself have opened. One I recall with a bitter memory was the Lytham Cricket Club Open Day With Side Shows And Swings. For over seven weeks a local clergyman had badgered me to perform the ceremony, which entailed standing on a makeshift podium created with two barrels and a plank, and squarking to a heap of toffee-daubed truants and zombie-like parents. As, on the day, I reached the Gardens, the heavens came apart under a deluge of whipped rain, and an old lady (this book wallows with them, by the way) came across to me, prodded me with a Dickensian umbrella and growled: 'It never rained when Vera Lynn opened it.'

That was only the start. The clergyman gave me a glass of mauve sherry, and through a megaphone thundered: 'I'd like to thank Mr Dawson for opening our fete today. I'm extremely grateful to him, because none of the big stars could do it.' As I began my address, a baleful tot threw an ice cream cornet at me and struck my hairline. This caused me to fall off the plank and my trousers split wide open. It was a sight that an elated gentleman later told me was 'like a peach under a pelmet'. At first I was nonplussed by the remark, until, with a digital exploration, I realized that my naked buttocks were in full view.

Enough of my anatomy; let us proceed down Clifton Drive and, veering at the White Church to the left, amble along the sea front from Granny's Bay to Fairhaven Lake.

The Bay is not really a place for the young ones, it is a place for those who have lived through times long gone. When night falls in the summer months, the sunsets are a tribute to the Greatest Architect of them all, and the lapping waters bring forth a nostalgia that is gleaned from an age that will never return. There is a story, an emotive one, about the Bay that calls up echoes from a long-departed era . . .

It was in the spring of 1894 that a beautiful maiden strolled along the sands skirting the Bay and dutifully exercised her two poodles. Her lover, a dashing subaltern from the 4th Hussars, embraced her and placed an engagement ring upon her finger. They kissed; his colourful tunic playing a backcloth to her crinolines, as their bodies intertwined in passion. Suddenly, from a small guest house where the subaltern was in residence, hobbled a servant carrying a message for the young soldier. He perused the note and

his face grew grave, for the message instructed him to rejoin his regiment due to sail to India, to quell an uprising in Nepal. Wildly and tearfully, they abandoned themselves to each other, and with great difficulty the subaltern tore himself away from his beloved and ran back to the guest house without a glance backwards. The maiden flung her arms out in anguish and the engagement ring flew off her finger and into the sand. In vain she searched for the ring, but to no avail . . . the ring was lost. Last year, at the age of a hundred and six, the once-beautiful maiden returned to the scene. Yes, you have guessed, her lover never returned from Nepal; he died leading a sortie into the foothills held by the rebels. She of course never married, and her journey to Granny's Bay was her final gesture before the Grim Reaper beckoned her. As her nurse trundled her along in her wheelchair, the memory of that day came back: the spring warmth, the excited poodles, her handsome lover . . . the parting. Just then, her wheelchair struck a large stone buried in a mound of sand, and as the chair began to topple over, she threw out her hand to save herself. Her hand sank into the sand, and lo and behold! It fell on dog shit.

That got you, hey? Well, it makes a change. I mean, where would we be without a laugh? Here.

Just a few yards on we arrive at Fairhaven Lake, with its cafés and gift stalls. There is something about Fairhaven Lake. Oh, there are bigger ones and deeper ones, but I don't think you will find one as pretty. Small islands break up the expanse of dark water, and ducks and drakes and disdainful swans glide past your skiff or motor boat and barely glance at you. Small boys fall in it as they propel their toy boats about, and elderly ladies hurl lumps of fossilized Hovis to waddling ganders. It is my firm belief that a sea creature lurks in the depths, and will one day drag my wife's mother down into a cavern and give itself indigestion off her mountainous chins.

St Anne's St Anne's-on-Sea is a dowager who refuses to come to terms with anything remotely modern. St Anne's is still tea dances and lavender and swooning maidens in odd gazebos. From Fairhaven Lake to the battered pier, the long promenade with its rockery walks and waterfalls is desperate for the swish of crinolines and the tattoo of sword sticks. All the large houses and hotels that form the boundary of the Inner Promenade are built with pre-war rustic brick and seasoned timber that doesn't crack every time a nail is driven through it. These houses and guest watering-holes look upon the putting greens that lie in front of the aforementioned rockery through heavily leaded windows reminiscent of hooded eyelids.

There are some concessions to the fact that young people actually exist. A miniature railway puffs dejectedly in a circle, and sagging trampolines wait for stolid children to jump up and down on them. St Anne's abounds in stout benches for old citizens to sit and stare, and all that's missing is a suicide booth. Wait a minute, that's unkind. St Anne's may not be the playground of the Western World, but it does have something to offer: peace and quiet . . . and there's nothing I like better than a little piece on the quiet.

St Anne's pier isn't really a pier any more. A fire destroyed most of it, and blackened wood and twisted iron leer at the unwary. Years ago, the pier had a theatre on the end of it, where great music hall acts performed: the masked Gurkhas and Winnie, underwater jugglers and rabbit benders, Faggot Poo and his Catholic Geese – we will never see their likes again.

The main square in St Anne's is truly majestic, and expensive. The buildings are Victorian and aloof, and appear to sneer at you if you haven't got a fur coat on (in St Anne's, the ladies wear furs during heatwaves). Some elderly matrons in the summer months stagger about, laden with gold trinkets and vast ermine wraps that startle you into thinking giant rodents are crawling towards you. There is in St Anne's an air of pretentiousness that often spoils what can be a very dignified resort, but smile at it all, and soon you fall under the magic of the place.

There are other fine things in the area. I myself am a member of a club that is wholly masculine; no women are allowed in. Within the premises of our male enclave are comfy leather chairs and snooker tables, bridge tables and drinking tables and tables for dominoes. Only once in living memory has a female actually got through the doors, and the incident, dreadful that it was, is still talked of when good men and true huddle together and drink to oblivion.

To the rear of St Anne's, away from the sea that is, lies the back road into Blackpool, and in this boggy countryside live hardy folk who are known locally as 'Moss Hogs'. They sell plants and flowers and things for the garden mostly, and they seldom ever seem to be there to serve you. Occasionally, you might glimpse one of them flitting through the mist, and when you do it's advisable to cross yourself and wear garlic.

But let's go back to the sea front, shall we? For holidaymakers of all ages, St Anne's does possess some fine hotels; all have indoor amusements and swimming pools; cabaret is performed nightly and they are all value for money. There is the Dalmeny Hotel, which caters for children as well as for adults, the St Ives and the Fern Lea, the Lindum and the Glendower – all excellent places for the tourist. Further along, expensive houses of unusual design gaze out to the sea and the flanking sandy beach, six miles long. Sand yachting is the famous sport of St Anne's and it is quite a spectacle, I must admit. Would you believe that St Anne's has a nature reserve? Well it has, and creeping about that reserve is a very rare type of sand fly. There, doesn't that make the pulses thump? God only knows what they look like, but bug-eyed botanists gather from all over the planet to glare at them.

Just yards away from the sand-fly nation one stumbles cross Pontin's. Ah, Pontin's! Surely half of the population was conceived in the chalets there. Holding your suitcases you voyage through the portals of the celebrated holiday camp and into a wonderland of illusion, all inclusive. Bright young men and women with fierce smiles grab you and pummel you into enjoying yourself. Parents can ditch their offspring and scurry away into bars whilst the kids mess about in high glee. You eat in enormous dining canteens that can bring back bitter memories for any man who did his bit in the forces, for Pontin's is a sort of covered-in Dunkirk. At the end of a fortnight there, you need a holiday to get over the holiday, but never mind – it's All Inclusive.

An ex-friend of mine, who shall be nameless because of the laws pertaining to libel, once talked me into judging a beauty competition for Miss Pontin. Being a person who has always admired feminine meat and the way it is packaged, I heartily agreed, little knowing that my 'friend' had already picked the winner, a lass from Widnes who in return for the title of Miss Pontin had agreed to shower physical gratitude upon my friend's fair body. After a few drinks I cared not who won the thing and onto the podium I stalked, bubbling with bonhomie and gin. Pretty girls by the parcel swayed

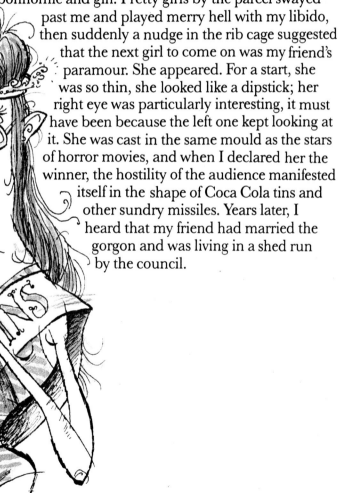

past me and played merry hell with my libido, then suddenly a nudge in the rib cage suggested that the next girl to come on was my friend's paramour. She appeared. For a start, she was so thin, she looked like a dipstick; her right eye was particularly interesting, it must have been because the left one kept looking at it. She was cast in the same mould as the stars of horror movies, and when I declared her the winner, the hostility of the audience manifested itself in the shape of Coca Cola tins and other sundry missiles. Years later, I heard that my friend had married the gorgon and was living in a shed run by the council.

BLACKPOOL TO HEYSHAM

Often dirty, always vulgar, seething with paper-hatted youths, drunks, crooks, ladies of easy virtue ... Yes, Blackpool is all of that but if you can accept the resort for what it is, then Blackpool will seem a magical place, for it is, at least, honest unto itself.

As you progress along South Shore, broad and open with a hint of the Roman Forum in the sea-front arches and pillars, you arrive at the Pleasure Beach. It is the largest pleasure centre in Europe, and its garish facade beckons you into its colourful maw like a gaily painted harlot.

Here are machines to throw you up into the sky, machines that hurtle you into black tunnels, machines that attempt to tear your tripes into shreds ... There are metal carts that whizz you round in thunderous twists and circles; helter skelters; big dippers; small dippers; water craft and aerial carriages designed to make you bring back the fish-and-chip supper you devoured the night before. There is noise, constant noise – of machinery grinding, carousel music, pop music from the teeming transistors carried by green-haired striplings. And smells – of hot toffee and candy floss, of sweat and overworked urinals. The shriek of a bloated robot clown battles against the shouts of the barkers: 'Roll up, roll up!' It becomes a dirge to the ears as you push your way through the densely packed regiments of visitors. Screams from the Ghost Train, laughter from the Wild Mouse, it's a nightmare of entertainment that buffets the senses. In this unreal world there is something for everyone – for bobbing racing swaying children; for heated children; for lost children and over-excited children. For open-mouthed girls sat in booths, thrilling to the words of a Romany palmist. For young men in tight trousering who thrust out genitalia in the hope of securing a scented conquest on the night-time sands.

For old couples putting coins into whirring machines. Even for young couples holding wet crying bundles, and skirting pools of vomit that lie like reproach outside refreshment halls. Everyone comes to the Pleasure Beach.

But Where Are The Giant Rats Of Bangalore? We have finally reeled back outside, there to inhale the rich mixture of ozone and chip fat. The Chip, symbol of all that is noble in Blackpool. Everywhere, lips suck on chips, blow on chips, chew on chips; the acrid stenches of vinegar and corner-shop perfume make an uneasy alliance in the salty air as we trundle up the promenade, past the bingo stalls and rock stands. On, ever on, the vista is the same.

Many things have changed since I first became acquainted with what was then known as the Golden Mile. Then there were side shows and, for a piffling sum, you were dragooned into a stygian gloom to look horrified upon the Two Headed Woman of Sumatra, or the Giant Rat of Bangalore. 'See the Snake Man,' a W. C. Fields-type voice would yell as you milled around in confusion. It was all a symphony of sight, smell and wonder. Now, the booths are gone; in their place, emporiums have sprung up which house hordes of fruit machines and Space Invader cabinets, whose function is to hypnotize schoolboys.

The Lancashire Babel
Blackpool Tower looms ahead, thrusting its iron crown into the heavens. Below, in the Tower building which forms the base, are yet further helpings of something for everyone. A circus, parrots, apes and

haggard lions . . . There are kiddie shows, and beer for the men. There are shops to buy souvenirs from, and gallons of tea for footsore ladies. It takes an age to see everything there is to see in the Tower, but impatient tourists make for the elevators that transport them to the top of the Lancashire Babel. Once up aloft, the wind bludgeons you and robs you of breath, and you're damn glad to get down. Oh, I admit the view is superb: Fleetwood to Preston can be clearly perceived if the climate is right; but all in all, the spectacle of Blackpool seen from above is an anti-climax, less compelling than the real-life uproar at ground level.

Night Falls Night falls and Blackpool regathers its energy. The pubs begin to overflow, the casinos, cafés and clubs fill up, and crowds sing in the streets. There will be street brawls and the police will be kept on the tips of their truncheons. I have played many clubs in Blackpool, and well recall the times when I was so far down on the bill, the only people who used my name were dogs. They were tough too; not the dogs, the clubs. I once foolishly asked an audience in a hellhole called Jenk's Bar what they would like me to do as an encore; to a man they replied: 'Stick the microphone up yer arse.'

Of course, the theatres in Blackpool are famous for the artistes who have performed in them. I myself, I might modestly add, have played them all: The Opera House, which is so big the mice walk about with St Christopher medals; the North Pier, a fine room for comedians, worth a visit if you have the stamina to force your way down the pier when a gale is blowing; Central Pier, where now Old Tyme Music Hall reigns supreme, was the scene of my biggest laugh – I fell off the stage and crushed the organ. Alas, Blackpool Grand is no more; memories of that theatre rush in, especially the one where the usherette seduced me in the dressing-room, more precisely on the rim of the sink . . . for months I suffered from a porcelain rash.

Every big name in the business has appeared in Blackpool at one time or another, and also smaller artistes like Enrico Higgins, the electric leg whistler from Halifax. He did very well until one night he blew a fuse and shorted his orchestrations. Who can forget Miriam Alroyd, the Jenny Lind of Selkirk? She used to sing 'Nearer My God To Thee' and do a striptease in a bucket of ferrets. She lost one of her ferrets one night, but she had a hell of a smile on her face.

Bide-A-Wee Nowhere else in the world has so many tyrannical boarding-house landladies, whose every word is law. One magnificent example of the breed ran a neo-Nazi training centre called Glen Haven. She was an amazon with so many double chins, it looked as if her head was resting on a pile of crumpets. When she was arrested for arson, her boarding house was found to be full of corpses of holidaymakers who had asked for more. A spinster from Swinton, who begged for a lump of parkin, was discovered in a tea chest with a sabre wound in her throat. A lonely vicar stayed there a week, and suffered shotgun burns on the buttocks as he tried to throw an SOS through a lavatory window. (Well, I like to think it could happen.)

The romance of Blackpool boarding houses lay in the names that were given to them by their proud proprietors. Hovels in back streets were called Bide-A-Wee, and gaunt grey shacks rejoiced in such titles as Casa Del Splendido and Astoria Riviera. One that I recall had a perpetual smell of cabbage on the stairs and a landlady with a drink problem. That superb dwelling was known as Shore View Hotel, and it was hidden behind a tram shed. The only way you could actually see the shore was by lying on top of a wardrobe with your neck craned to the left.

Blackpool also has some quite high-class hotels. The Imperial on North Shore, a massive Victorian edifice, is good value for money. My favourite hotel, though, is the celebrated Norbeck Castle. God only knows who its architect was, but he must have a been a psychedelia freak. The place looks like the worst of Camelot crossed with a Tunisian massage parlour; on the other hand, it does have a bottomless swimming pool and some ideal bars.

Salty Fleetwood When you leave Blackpool, going north, you pass through residential Bispham, then Cleveleys, a smaller resort very popular with tourists of all ages that caters well for drunks like unto myself. We find ourselves looking at Rossall School, a fine tutorial heap that has disgorged many great men such as Callum Smallpiece, the celebrated traveller and bankrupt, who went to Holland and opened a mountaineering school there. Callum was born at an early age which was a godsend to his parents because it meant he fitted his pyjamas. His wife used to be the leader of a strike picket outside a chickenpox vaccine factory; when she caught the disease she became the first picket that was ever pocked.

Fleetwood looms ahead – a growing resort thanks to its fishing industry and passenger shipping. Fleetwood will also become an important container base for the oil that one day will be sucked up from the sea. I like Fleetwood. The fish market is supreme: you can buy cod the size of a sperm whale and herrings that melt in the mouth. The town is always busy, and one can imagine old salts stumping about on mahogany legs with parrot droppings on their shoulders. The beer is good in Fleetwood, I might add, and there is night life a-plenty in the pubs.

Before we board the ferry that will take us to Knott End on the far side of the River Wyre, let us savour some of the place names that dot this attractive peninsula ... Little Thornton, Four Lane Ends, Singleton, Trunnah, Staining, Hardhorn and Elswick; Poulton-le-Fylde, Thistleton and Inskip, where tall radio masts belonging to the Royal Navy monitor every ship in every corner of the world. Are you impressed? Well, you should be, because Lancashire is all things to all diversities. Lancashire is one of the largest dairy producers in the world, and the Fylde is one of the most prolific areas for cattle breeding; on a hot summer's day the aroma of fresh dung is a tonic to city lungs.

We are now across the River Wyre, which is a fast tidal water flow with dangerous currents to trap the unwary. Seth Plumm, the well known horse strangler and cat piles specialist, once shot the eyebrows off a trout in this river with a metal crossbow and was given a week's free lodgings in a windmill.

Beauteous Expanses Knott End is now defunct as a seaside resort, but in Victorian times it was a sort of 'in-place' for sprightly mashers and ladies of the chorus. My Great Aunt Maud was the last of the Gaiety Girls in Edwardian London; men used to throw roses at her as she danced and later they would drink champagne from her slipper ... she was seventy-nine when she died with damp feet and greenfly.

Again, we are faced with quaint place names that are peculiar to this area of Lancashire: Pilling, Preesall, Stalmine, Cockerham Moss, England Hill ... Across the Shard Bridge we drop into Hambleton and meander through thicketed lanes to St Michael's-on-the-Wyre. The church of St Michael's is steeped in antiquity, and the lead is still on the roof. The rolling landscape of Lancashire is seen at its finest as you journey towards Longridge and on to the Trough of Bowland, surely one of the most beauteous expanses in the world (of which more later).

Magnificent pubs abound in Goosnargh and Wood Plumpton, Catforth and Wharles, and cosy eating places where one can purchase savoury olde Northern dishes such as Mole pie and steamed owl's elbows. Try a visit to Garstang, and eat well at the Tythe Barn, where the odour of freshly baked bread plays hell with your sinuses. You can enjoy Poulton-le-Fylde's celebrated German Clock Festival, held every week unless there is a Friday in it. At midday, all pedestrians stop walking and a hunched Prussian, a former traffic warden, asks you to shake your head from side to side and mutter 'Tick-tock'. If you find difficulty in saying 'tock' because of faulty dentures, he will grasp you in a half-nelson and shout: 'I have ways and means of making you tock!'

There is a part of the Lancashire coast that is filled with mystery: well, to me at any rate. It is the region past Glasson, through Overton and around to Morecambe. Even the sea looks shifty here, and the sands are menacing as we trot towards Heysham, where they make that wonderful brew, nettle beer. Nettle beer . . . ah! What nectar indeed, only be careful with it, otherwise you can finish up with a bladder full of thistles.

Legend has it that off Yeomans Bank there are sunken galleons a-plenty, but to date nowt has been found of any value. Just to the north is the Lake District, vast areas of which come under the jurisprudence of Lancashire, although the new boundaries have placed them in Cumbria. We Lancastrians refute this, and one day will ask for Home Rule – and invade Flookburgh if our demands are not met.

Once more I shall have to deviate from the plot. My wife in a rare moment of sobriety has asked me for details of the above-mentioned Mole pie and steamed owl's elbows – what an example of appalling culinary ignorance. For the sake of peace, I will outline the recipe:
1 Take one elderly mole with bad feet.
2 Cross its ankles until it whistles 'Swanee'.
3 Stand the owl on its ear and cover with lentils.
4 Add a pinch of braised cabbage and kipper fat.
5 Kick it up a motorway until flat and boil.
6 Steam out the wrinkles and serve in a warm hat.

They don't make food like they used to; it's no

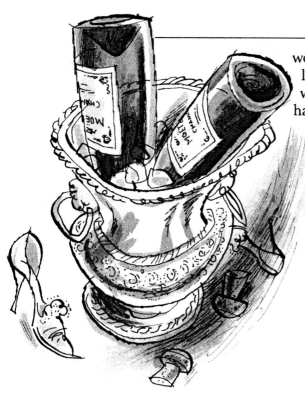

wonder that Giggleswick Harry lived to be over twenty-three in wet weather. Where the hell am I? Let's have a look at Lancaster, shall we? Dear old Lancaster; a venerable historic mound with a magnificent cathedral, and several sons of whom it is inordinately proud.

MEN OF LANCASTER

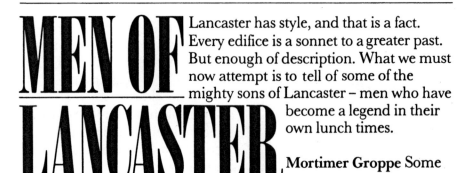

Lancaster has style, and that is a fact. Every edifice is a sonnet to a greater past. But enough of description. What we must now attempt is to tell of some of the mighty sons of Lancaster – men who have become a legend in their own lunch times.

Mortimer Groppe Some years ago, as I warmed myself in front of a log fire in the Explorers Club in Old Lancaster, the name of Groppe entered the conversation. I remember the night well: I had just asked the waiter for a large port, and he had given me a photograph of Liverpool.

'Fine man, Groppe.' Thus spake a voice from a late arrival, one Herbert Fish, who as you may recall once lifted a lorry load of tripe out of a bog and, in so doing, broke his pelvis. The story now recounted by Fish filled me with pride for my fellow Lancastrian.

In the June of '99 Mortimer Groppe discovered the tomb of the Pharaoh Ram in the Valley of the Ox near a culvert in Suez. Above the slab of stone that concealed the entrance to the tomb were these words: 'For it is written in the Lost Book of The Old Ones that he who

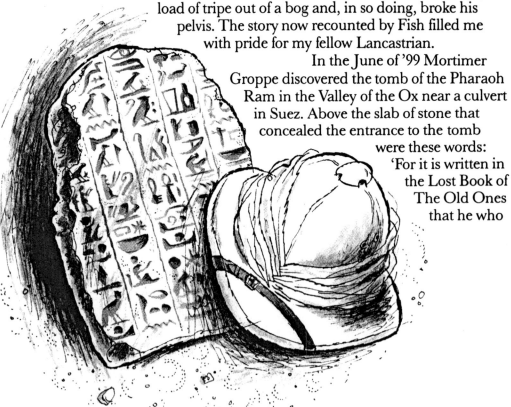

defiles the sacred chamber of the Mighty Ram will be cursed with dismemberment.'

Groppe ignored the warning and he entered the tomb whistling the hit song 'Boiled Beef And Carrots.' Mortimer's find made him famous and he had crumpets with Lady Astor. Three months later, at a dinner thrown in his honour, his leg fell off, and from that day on every member of his family lost a leg at the age of forty-three. His daughter Ada found that her leg was coming loose at a Scrabble party, and sure enough on the way home . . . it fell off and went down a grid. She was a brave lass and got a job making hops for the brewery, but sadness clouded her grit as she confided to her father: 'Oh, daddy, I'll never get married, no man will take me on now that I only have one leg.' Mortimer Groppe jumped across to his offspring, put his arm around her shoulder and said with a deep love in his tone: 'Fear not, owd lass, one day you'll be hopping down the main road and you will meet your Prince Charming – and he'll sweep you off your foot.'

Aza Gartside Born in a flat over a blouse factory in Lancaster, Aza was abandoned by his parents at the age of fifty-two in a permissive launderette. Always a religious man, he went to the Congo Delta to sell health foods to cannibals. It was, by any standard, a most hazardous trek. In my possession I have a portion of his diary, which I feel grips the reader with a sense of the torment he endured.

'Monday 8th August 1889
Hacking our way through the dark undergrowth, bitten by swarms of mosquitoes, three of my native bearers died this morning of beri-beri; we buried them. On and on we struggle; the heat, oh, the burning heat.

Tuesday 9th August 1889
Attacked by a rampant pigmy with dysentery. I have to shoot him; forgive me, O Lord. Apes invade our encampment and they have eaten my cucumber sandwiches. The heat, always the torrid sun beating down on my pith helmet.

Wednesday 10th August 1889
Half-day closing.'
Aza vanished in early September whilst trying to sell nut fritters to a tribe that lived in trees. All that was found at his last camp was a pair of braces, a set of teeth and a strong smell of chutney. Aza Gartside

may have been foolhardy, but as his ex-wife Mary said just before she opened a cement works: 'I can only hope he went down well.'

Howard Clockbottom Lancaster also produced a fine music hall artiste. Yes, my dear reader, we must never forget Howard Clockbottom, the pig's trotter impressionist and comedy balloonist. He played before the Duke Of York, the Queen, and some other pubs in Blackburn. Alas! He went slightly peculiar and married a horse.

Harry Hargreaves Not all Lancaster men were so physical. One, in particular, became a great philosopher. You instantly know, of course, to whom I refer – Harry Hargreaves, no less.

Hargreaves had an unhappy childhood. His father worked in a cotton mill and one day he got dragged into his loom and warped his weft. His mother, who played piano in a marching band, took an overdose of castor oil and shot herself. Hargreaves, now an orphan, was brought up by his maiden aunt and it was from her that he gleaned his love of literature. It is, I suppose, a tribute to the maiden aunt that her influence helped to broaden Harry's already not-inconsiderable intellect, and at the age of only twenty-five he became a don at Oxford. Harry was a thin man, indeed rumour had it that when he went for an x-ray, the doctor had to bend him double to get a picture, and on one occasion he fell through a string vest.

In 1906 his thesis was published. It was entitled: 'If a man has no children then his son won't have any either.' It created a storm amongst the intelligentsia, and bricks were thrown through his greenhouse. Society shunned him and he became a hermit in his back garden, living in a box.

The advent of World War One brought him back into prominence and he moved to a bigger box. He firmly believed that kids who lived in Berlin picked up the German language quicker than, say, a kid who lived in Giggleswick; somebody gave him a medal. He never smoked or drank; he avoided fatty foods and he never went with women, and eventually he died of nothing.

His theories live on, however, and we are the richer for them.

THE WILD COUNTRY

The countryside that abounds around the central Lancashire towns of Blackburn and Darwen is one of yawning moorland with ancient stone walls breaking up the faceless stretches of the bleak hills, where only ragged sheep roam. There is a savage and yet forlorn aspect about the broad Lancashire moorlands, as if the fight to keep away the encroachment of industry has finally wearied the thin topsoil into allowing the rock strata beneath to expose its slate-grey chest, to blacken under sullen skies.

We are like our landscapes. Soft and often sad; sometimes as harsh as the mighty Pennines, sometimes as friendly as the puppy that rummages in the back-street gutters.

It was on a farm, high above the smoky contours of Darwen, that I, at the age of sixteen, fell in love with a winsome maid of fourteen summers. Her hair was a tangled wreath of dark curls that she was wont to toss in anger at some imagined slight. Her eyes, so brown and wide, flecked with green tints, held my adolescent heart in bondage, and I tried with all my powers to become part of her country life.

Being city-born, the task was not easy. Animals terrified me, and a mere glance from a cow was sufficient to cause me to leap behind a barn. What was I doing on the farm in the first place? You might well ask. I had left school at the tender age of fourteen, and at that time jobs were none too easy to obtain; someone suggested that farming could be the answer for a restless lad, and so, after answering an advertisement in the labour exchange for a temporary hand to help around the farm in return for food and shelter and a small wage, I found myself co-existing with cattle and poultry and the smell of mixed droppings. There, too, I fell in love with the farmer's daughter. Eeh, lad, she taught me more about life than I bargained for. She used to play a game with me behind the sheep pen; I don't know what it was called, but cricket never had a chance after that.

In my effort to win her approval, I tried my hand at milking a cow. For ages I messed about trying to get milk, to no avail, but the creature seemed to be really enjoying my fumbling efforts.

The love of my life stood watching me intently as I pulled and tugged. 'I'm not very good at this,' I crowed. 'But by hell she seems to be very happy about it.' My sweet one nodded and said: 'I'm not surprised, you're milking the bull.' I left soon after; the bull wanted to get engaged.

SONG OF BOWLAND

To see Lancashire in its unspoilt state, go through Chipping and marvel at the Norman church, then beetle on to Longridge Fell and be in awe of the majestic sweep of moorland and forest. Remember, too, that you are only a few miles from industrial towns.

Ere long we find ourselves in delightful Bolton-by-Bowland. It was there, one summer's eve, that I experienced a most moving emotion.

I recall that I had sat myself down on a heap of boulders with a packet of tinned salmon sandwiches and a bottle of ale that I had culled from a pub called The Three Fishes, a lovely old inn situated in the village of Mitten near Clitheroe. The summer dusk, with all the familiar smells and drones, enveloped my shoulders; darting wild life quivered in the thickets; the chuckle of a

secret brook accompanied the trills of impatient robins, and nearby a Mini rocked as two ardent lovers went at it like frogs up a pump.

Suddenly, the tranquillity was disturbed by the sound of a long-drawn-out chord on a violin. A man appeared from behind a bush wearing a long mackintosh tied together by string around his disreputable figure. There was an air of melancholy about him as he placed the violin under the stubble on his chin, a suggestion of hopelessness in his manipulation of the bow. Frankly, I confess that I tensed myself, fearing that the man might be unbalanced and assail me with his instrument.

I need not have feared, for he played a lament upon the violin that soon had tears welling unbidden to my eyes as the sad notes trembled on the warm air. How long he played, I know not, but when the last sombre chord died, I found that I was holding my breath in exquisite anticipation.

I walked slowly towards him and he eyed my progress with a fleeting apprehension. 'My good sir,' I said almost in a whisper. 'Pray tell me the name of that most haunting melody, for it made my senses reel with its harmonic beauty.' There was a silence, then he spoke. 'Thank you, sir. I'm glad you liked it. I made it up, you see.' 'Do you mean to tell me that you composed that musical rapture?' said I with astonishment. He nodded. 'Have you had it published?' I asked him. He shook his unkempt head shyly and replied: 'No sir, I've tried, but nobody will touch it.'

Anger stormed through my every fibre. 'Give me your manuscript my friend,' I said. 'I will take it to the songsmiths of Charing Cross Road, and I will use what influence I have to ensure that the world shall hear of your music.' Trustingly he handed me a grubby manuscript that smelled strongly of chips, then he turned on his scuffed heels and started to walk back to the bush. 'Wait a minute,' I shouted. 'What is the tune called?' He poked his head out of the bush and said: 'It's called "I love you so much I break wind".'

Speaking of tunes, was it not a Lancashire man who wrote the song that kept our feet a-tapping through the dark days of Dunkirk? Do you remember it?

'There was a young man from Bombay
Who sailed to China one day.
He was strapped to the tiller
With a sex-starved gorilla,
And China's a bloody long way.'

INTERLUDE

I've put the typewriter away for a moment and I'm enjoying a reflective cheroot, and thinking about this and that; mostly that. The Lancashire weather is superb: warm and all-embracing, in fact one hardly notices the rain.

My wife is in the kitchen making the evening meal; I can hear the fire extinguisher going. I'm not saying she burns everything, but we lay the table with an altar cloth. I bought her a pressure cooker once, I don't know what she did with it but she managed to put a turnip into orbit. Like most modern women, my wife is obsessed with fancy cooking. Tonight she's threatened us with Chicken Kiev; the last time she did that dish, I threw a piece of it to our dog and he spent the rest of the night with a paw down his throat.

Why, oh why, won't she stick to what we are familiar with? Elsewhere in this book I mention Lancashire food – *several* times. Why can't I ever get any? If we go out for a meal, it's the same; she always wants Chinese. Mind you, I'll say one thing for the wife: we don't have any mice in the kitchen – the rats have ate them all. You can even eat off our floor; you have to, the table's filthy.

Every Christmas Day for the last seven years we've had the wife's mother up for dinner. This year we're having a change . . . I'm going to let her in.

She is as bad as her daughter at cooking. She tried to do beans on toast once, but she clogged up the toaster when she poured the beans in.

I feel sorry for the father-in-law; the only time he opens his mouth is when he yawns. He is the thinnest man I've ever known, last week he threw himself onto the floor and missed it. Ah, the smoke in the kitchen is clearing, it's time for a gastronomic nightmare . . .

PART TWO
THE STUFF OF LEGENDS

ROOTS

Some years ago, I went through a traumatic period in my life. Nothing went well no matter how hard I tried, and then after years of married bliss my wife ran away with the fellow next door . . . and oh, I did miss him.

My soul became restless. I opted out of society and meandered through Lancashire in the fashion of a Romany. One fine night in the Forest of Rossendale I stumbled over a cairn of age-pitted stones, plummeted down a steep slope and found myself in a crouched position over a recumbent ram, which took great exception to my posture and bit me in a portion of my anatomy where I can ill afford the loss. At that most painful of moments, from behind a clump of groundsel, an elderly gentleman appeared, and as his gaze fell upon my prostrate form, he gave vent to a strangled cry, and sank to his knees in a gesture of humility. I scrambled to my feet and eyed the old chap warily. 'What's up?' I ventured to ask. In reply he pointed a shaking digit at the large hole in the seat of my trousers, and in particular at the birthmark on my right buttock, which is in the shape of a duck's foot (the birthmark, not my bum).

Then the elderly churl clasped his hands together and shouted: 'Sir Guy, you've come home.' The story that followed filled me with a sense of destiny . . .

It seems that in the spring of 1934, the old Duke of Potts Belching was having it away in a hay loft with a serving maid called Agnes. Suddenly, she threw the old Duke off her naked body; he hit his noble head on a brass fender and a rampant gander chewed his quivering backside with immense élan. The old Duke went quite ga-ga after the incident and finished up living in a windmill with an architect who wore a frock. Nine months later, at the height of the hunt ball at the stately home of the Potts Belchings, the french windows were flung open and, with the wind flying through her hair, there stood Agnes holding a damp bundle. 'Here is the true heir to the Potts Belching title!' screamed Agnes, and a retired solicitor set fire to himself with a Dunhill as she ripped at the swaddling clothes to disclose the slumbering infant beneath. Quite unintentionally, Agnes had been holding the bundle upside down, and what now thrust itself at the shocked squirearchy was a pair of wrinkled pink globes, one of which bore the unmistakeable duck's-foot imprint. After an initial stunned silence, the assembly made a grab at Agnes, but she escaped on a camel and fled the Forest of Rossendale forever.

For years, members of the Potts Belching family searched for a male child with a birthmark like a duck's foot on his bottom, but to no avail. Now, through a freak accident, I had returned, been recognized by an old family retainer, and could assert my right to inherit.

If any reader can therefore enlighten me as to the whereabouts of any surviving member of the Potts Belching family, I will gladly give ten per cent of whatever I may cop for, plus a chit guaranteeing a fortnight's free ale in Wigan.

A LANCASHIRE LOVE STORY

One dreamy summer, when the skies showed only a trace of vague nimbus and the woods and thickets gave a shadowed invitation as the benign sun poured thick warmth upon us, I came across an old thatched Tudor cottage whose black and white timbers groaned with the weight of antiquity. The small garden was a riot of roses that grew in jumbled confusion to the very edge of the stout front door.

I was in the quaint little village of Goosnargh, a few miles north from Preston on the road to Longridge Fell, a delightful place mentioned earlier in the context of magnificent pubs and cosy eating-places. But Goosnargh, and this very Tudor cottage, pluck at the heartstrings as well as the gut.

Within the cool confines of the cottage, a smell of freshly baked bread made heady the senses and the aroma jostled for attention with the scent of wild hyacinths. On the gnarled block of old timber that served as a mantelpiece above the rough stone fireplace, sat faded prints that paid homage to a bygone age. The walls were whitewashed and slatted with wooden strips, and here and there in no set pattern hung paintings and horse brasses. The cottage was the home of Mr and Mrs Albert Wormold, two elderly people with all the years of experience and life etched in their faces.

Theirs was a love story that no novelette could ever capture. In the spring of 1917, Albert returned from France, wounded in the hell that was the push to the Hindenburg Line. He stood alone amongst the hordes of soldiers at Manchester's Exchange Station, his wound throbbing, abated only by the relief he felt at coming alive out of the war.

His battle-weary eyes took in the trim and comely figure of a young nurse who was ushering broken men into lorries for dispatch to hospitals. The young nurse turned as if conscious of

Albert's scrutiny and a bond immediately joined them. Albert limped over to her and asked her name. It was Elsie, and she smiled as she told him.

Years later, Albert confessed that he didn't know what came over him, but at the moment they discovered each other, he plucked a strand of her golden hair, entwined it around a pound note and give it to a bookie's runner to wager on a horse. Elsie rummaged in her bag and produced a small bottle of whisky, and gave Albert a drink to wish him luck with his bet. The horse won, that night they embraced and within two weeks they were married. Taking a hair from Elsie's head became a tradition, and so too did the drinking of spirits for luck.

Today, they live in that lovely old cottage. They've been together for sixty-six years and they are as much in love now as they were back in 1917. If you should ever find yourself in Goosnargh, you'll see them there. You can't mistake them really – she's bald and he's pissed.

IS LANCASHIRE THE PROMISED LAND?

Many well-informed sources within the county firmly believe that one day Lancashire will break away from the rest of Britain and become a republic. Some militant Lancastrians want to see a deep moat dug all the way round the county's borders and filled with piranha fish. Frankly, I'm against this idea. For a start, it won't keep the Yorkists out; they'll simply eat the fish and the rates will go up.

The Swiss-born, Blackpool-based scientist Doctor Helmut Clack, whose book *How To Stretch A Coloured Headache* is considered by many to be a minor masterpiece, and is now on sale in Boots, told a conference of left-wing mindreaders that Lancashire should be jacked up twenty-four feet in the air and supported on rubber washers. In his view, this would save building a wall and the saving on bricks could go towards a holiday in Sweden.

At a secret meeting in a pub in Ramsbottom, General Pilgrim C. Fogg put forward the proposal that Lancashire should form a private army with its own band, and invade Whitehall during the last week in August. Miss Amelia Mogg agreed with the old General and they sang a sea shanty to an accordion. The Very Reverend Eric Fanshawe-Bluett, recently cleared on a charge of gross indecency with a masked cadet in a boathouse, said that there was evidence to suggest that Christ Himself had once sold deckchairs in Southport.

Speaker after speaker testified that Lancashire was a self-sufficient county and could well do without the rest of the country. That admirable Member of Parliament, Sir Henry Claymore, received a rapturous ovation when he spoke at length about the idea that Oldham Town Hall should become a permissive launderette and bridge club.

Lancashire 3 Roman Army 1 The fiercely independent spirit that shines through such radical ideas was not born in a day. More than two thousand years ago, the invading Romans were soon reduced to tears by the indomitable spirit of the Ancient Lancastrians.

After they had defeated the Iceni tribe, the Roman legions had little difficulty in marching northwards up Watling Street. Those indolent buffoons in the Midlands never even tried to stay the Roman invasion, they merely carried on making tea pots.

Some Cheshire pubs had signs up saying 'No Roman coaches', but in the main it would seem that they collaborated with the enemy, and even leased them a piece of waste ground on the banks of the River Dee where they built a Chester, which is Latin for 'fort' or 'camp'. From what one can gather, the fort was rather camp, and a lot of the troops carried a short sword with matching handbag.

Soon, the hellish legions were penetrating Lancashire and a main fort was established which became known as Manchester. Now, for the first time, the Romans started getting problems: the council wouldn't let them park their chariots in side streets, and the roads were always full of red cones. Then a campaign of sabotage took place. Umbrellas were tampered with, and the spokes cut halfway through, so that when the legions marched out on parade in the rain, the umbrellas fell to pieces and a lot of soldiers caught 'flu! This led to a drain on the National Health and Beecham's Powders went on the black market.

It was depressing for the Romans, who could not understand why the pubs closed early on Sundays. Worse was to come. Chip-shop owners started putting sweeteners in their cod steaks and, before long, Roman teeth were rotting away. Peronius, a centurion of the day, wrote to his mother in Naples begging her to see Augustus the Divine Caesar to ask him to send dentures over by the handful as his troops were no longer capable of chewing anything. The rascally Lancashire lads began selling yards of tripe to Roman soldiers, telling them they were overcoats, and soon the smell made a lot of the charioteers impotent and, in some cases, addicts for bingo.

On top of all that, it rained all the time; the metal skirts worn by the foot soliders started rusting up, and the lads couldn't pee. In a desperate bid to defeat the Lancastrians, Hadrian was sent over with an army of bricklayers, and told to build a wall across Lancashire. He hired a guide from a Chorley travel agency and, after promising him many gold talents, asked the guide to lead him to central Lancashire where he proposed to start erecting the wall. The guide, a sturdy Lancashire chap, whose sister had been ignored in a mass Roman gang bang, led the weary Hadrian through Lancashire and up to Scotland. The poet Marcus Auronius tells of Hadrian saying to the guide: 'Nil verum passagum quo?' Which, freely translated, means: 'Where the bloody hell are we?'

The guide's plan worked, and that is why Hadrian's

Wall is in the wrong place. When you think of it, it's ridiculous building a wall to keep the Scots out. All you needed to do was to hold Flag Day collections; that would have stopped them.

Glue On The Sandals The Roman occupation of Lancashire was in name only. Head colds and bad chests took the edge off the Roman troops and all they wanted to do was go to the pictures. One tactic used successfully by the Lancashire freedom fighters was to lure unwary Romans into a disused coal mine, where huge quantities of glue had been smeared on the floor. Once a soldier's sandals were stuck to the glue, big Lancashire lasses grabbed him and let starving moles bite him. This trick was so successful that a song was written about it; later it was stolen and sung by Harry Lauder:

'A Roman, in the glue-mine

With moles and lasses by yer side.'

Yes, it was the Lancastrians who really defeated the Roman Empire. However, like everything else, this great feat was covered up by politicians who were frightened of losing their package holidays in Italy. But you cannot hide the truth forever, and when independence comes to our shire, any Liberal who loses his deposit will be made to watch *Crossroads* in Scarborough.

So there you have it, a potted historical account of how the face of destiny was changed by determined men whose love of their heritage defeated a superior foe. Let Marcus Auronius have the honour of concluding this emotive tribute: 'Sic todum enemium mundo: Mancunium offereum'. That impassioned cry means: 'If they ever give the world an enema, they'll do it in Manchester.'

LANCASHIRE HEROES

Harold Many years ago there was a Clitheroe man who fished the River Hodder for the marvellous trout that swarm in the racing current of that meandering water. He was a solitary man, well liked by his fellow fishermen, but he did not court popularity. It therefore came as quite a shock to the local angling club, as well as to the man's neighbours, when it was discovered that he was a bigamist.

The case was heard in the Rochdale Assizes and the courtroom was jammed with the curious and those who had rubbed shoulders with the accused. It was a drama that not only is still talked about today, it was one that gave a new expression to the English language.

It appeared that the man, one Harold Ainsley, had unlawfully wed one Edith Jones from Blackburn, whilst still married to his first wife, Kate Ainsley, née Simpson, whose father was a noted ferret sexer from Clayton-le-Moors. Ainsley conducted his own defence and soon had the packed courtroom on his side with his flow of rhetoric.

'My Lord,' he intoned. 'This is a heartcry from a mere mortal who fell in love with two women, and loves them both. 'Tis not I who stands here accused, but the system that says a man can have only one wife. My Lord, let this trial change the face of justice, and allow a breath of fresh air into the marriage laws of this noble land.' The judge banged his gavel to restore order after the uproar that followed Harold's impassioned speech. Looking sternly at Harold, he clasped his hands together and in a voice full of rebuke said:

'Mr Ainsley, no matter how much sympathy one might feel for the obvious sincerity of your words, the law is the law, and that is a fact. Therefore I must find you guilty of bigamy and let me remind you once more . . . you simply cannot have your Kate and Edith.'

Sam In the snug inns of Edgworth and Holcombe Brook, they still recount the time-honoured legend of Sam Whipple, landlord of the Compass Inn, which lay above Ashworth Valley on the old Roman Road. Whilst attending a brewer's convention in Liverpool, Sam got drunk and fell across the railway line just outside Lime Street Station. An express from Carlisle hurtled down and severed Sam's head clean from his shoulders. At that moment, a Latvian immigrant in the guard's van saw what had happened and leapt from the speeding train. With great presence of mind he shoved Sam's head back on his shoulders and marched the unfortunate Whipple to the Liverpool Infirmary.

Alas, the surgeon informed the Latvian, despite his brave effort it was too late for Sam; the head could not be sewn back on. Just then, a nurse from Ghana who was studying the effects of malaria on tree frogs, mentioned that there was a sheep in the laboratory, ready for vivisection. Without consulting anyone, the surgeon immediately operated on both the sheep and Sam, and within an hour there was a sheep's head on Whipple's neck and the publican lived.

Sam sat up in his hospital bed eating his grass sandwiches and feeling a bit daft with his sheep's head, but as his wife said: 'Eeh, lad, tha's still with us and people will get used to your sheep's 'ead in time.' But every time Sam had a stroll around the hospital grounds, fellow patients took one look at him and started laughing, so he took to wearing a paper bag over his sheep's head. Finally the time came for Sam to go back home to his pub, but he wasn't looking forward to it. His wife reassured him: 'Sam, lad,' she said fondly. 'All the customers know what's happened, and they'll welcome you home with open arms.'

They arrived back at the Compass. The pub had been decorated with flags and bunting, and Sam began to relax . . . until he got inside. As soon as the customers saw his sheep's head, they started roaring with laughter, and so Sam did the only thing he could do. He 'baaahed' them.

Seth If you sit sometimes in the Old Links Golf Club at St Anne's-on-Sea, and you ply enough of the older members with pints of Boddingtons bitter, they may open up and tell you the legend of Seth Hollingworth who played that course every day of his life until he fell ill at the ripe old age of ninety-eight.

He wasn't a bad player from all accounts, but one hole eluded his efforts completely ... the sixteenth. For fifty-three years that hole had never seen his ball go down it. Often it went near, but never 'plop', down it. One day he'd hook the ball into the woods near it, another day he'd slice it into a pond; he never succeeded in actually holing out. It made him an angry man and he became morose and given to talking to himself. In the clubhouse, he would sup his ale and mutter to the fireplace, then heave himself up and march to the sixteenth and try to putt a ball down. Never.

On the other holes he was a more-than-average golfer and did quite well in competitions, that is, until he reached the dreaded sixteenth, and then he would tremble and make a mess of his game.

The years rolled on and Seth staggered into his dotage and many of his relatives wanted him put away, as by now he had got into the habit of standing over the hole for hours at a stretch and cursing it to high heaven. Finally, Seth lay dying. His wife Annie mopped his fevered brow as the old man clutched his putter in his veined old hands.

Annie said: 'Is there owt Ah can do for thee, Seth? You haven't got long, love, and the boiled ham for the funeral 'as been ordered.' Seth gazed at her and he said slowly: 'Aye, lass, tha' can do summat for me. Have me cremated and put me ashes down the sixteenth 'ole. What I failed to do in life, I'll succeed in death.' When Seth had gone to the big Caddie-in-the-Sky, Annie dutifully had him cremated and, under an archway of No 3 irons, she walked up to the sixteenth hole, knelt, opened the lid of the urn ... and the wind blew him out of bounds.

Red For years and years the old Red Indian had sat perched on a rocky slope in the heart of Beatrix Fell; a blanket round his shoulders, his profile thrown against the skyline like a copper coin. Rumour had it that he had once been part of a Wild West show that had toured Lancashire at the turn of the century; but nobody could be sure of it, although he was certainly a great age.

His late rise to fame started one summer's day, when a farmer stopped to have a chat with him. 'Nice day,' said the farmer. The Indian unfolded his arms and ducked his head inside his blanket. A minute later he withdrew it and replied: 'Sun go in soon ... winds light and variable bring rain.' The farmer scoffed, but an

hour later it rained like hell and one of his bullocks drowned in a bog.

The farmer told everybody about what the Indian had forecast, and before long all the local farmers were consulting the aged savage. He was always accurate. Some days he would poke his head under his blanket and re-emerge and state: 'Cold Nor' west wind it come with snow flurry'; or 'Hot spell brought on by ridge of pressure from Shetlands, this will not last, there will be frost on high ground.'

They flocked from all over the country to ask his advice about the weather and he never let them down. In Alberta, Canada, a cattle rancher was about to set out to trek a giant herd to Seattle in the United States, and he was desperate to find out what conditions would be like for the journey. He'd heard of Lancashire's old Indian and he decided to make a trip to Beatrix Fell to ask the Indian about the weather prospects.

At last he sat at the feet of the noble savage, and spoke earnestly to him. 'Please, sir, tell me what the weather will be like in Canada for the month of October?'

The Indian dived under his blanket and when he looked up again, his face was very grave: 'I cannot tell you what weather like any more,' he said sadly. The rancher was dumbstruck. 'Do you mean you have lost your powers?' he asked. The Indian shook his head. 'Battery in radio no good.'

Owd Tommy Up on Calder Fell, when the moon sweeps a beam across the yawning acres of grassland, a visitor may chance to come in contact with Owd Tommy, the shepherd from remote Whitewell. He is often to be found standing alone with his dog, simply gazing at the night sky and drawing deeply on his battered briar. Owd Tommy has been on the Fell longer than most people can recall and everyone respects his word; that is why, when he talks of the time he encountered a space visitor, one is compelled to believe him.

But let him tell it in his inimitable style, and judge for yourself the credibility of the tale:

'Ah was sat in my cottage having three pennorth from't chip oil (chip shop) when sudden like, Ah saw a bright flash of light streak towards me cottage. Fearing as if it might be a bolt o' lightning, I rushed outside, just in time to see a ball of fire crash on top o' me 'en 'ut. Frankly, I'd seen nobbut (nothing) like it see, and when I thowt to me sen (thought to myself) tha'd best get a peeler (policeman, nicknamed after Sir Robert Peel, a Lancashire man who formed the police force as we know it today) it was as if summat 'ad 'eard me, for out of the fiery ball came a ladder and down it climbed a tall thin feller.

'He were green all over and he had one eye in't middle of his napper (head) and he kept jumpin' up and down an' twisting his legs. "Hello," I said, "have thee cum from't Moon?" The Thing shook its head and the ears wiggled. "Have thee cum from Mars, then?" I asked it. Again it shook its head and kept wriggling its legs and jumpin! Ah got a bit fed up wi' it. I said: "Alreet lad, where've thee cum from?" The Thing stared at me and said in a funny voice: "Venus. Millions of miles from Earth." Ah said: "Eeh bah gum, that's a long way to travel in such a tiny ball, what can I do for thee?" And the Thing said to me: "Can I please use your toilet?"'

Billy Criminals in Manchester, and we do have a few I must confess, often talk about Billy 'The Fox' Marsden, reckoned by all the underworld to be the unluckiest crook in history. Nothing ever went right for Billy; he stole some bananas once and, when he peeled them, they were empty.

One day, in Market Street, he was on the point of attempting a smash-and-grab raid on a jeweller's window, when he was arrested for stealing the brick he had in his hand.

He was very short-sighted, and when he held anybody up, he used to snarl 'Stick 'em up . . . are they up?' So poor was his eyesight, he finished up picking pockets in a nudest camp. Yes, he really was touching the bottom.

Perhaps his greatest gaffe was the time he attempted to rob a bank in Daisy Nook. He donned a mask, pulled out a gun and entered the swing doors of the local branch of Barclay's. As the door revolved, his toe got stuck under the rubber rim of the door; Billy fell, his mask flew off and he went sliding across the highly polished floor of the bank on his back, and his gun became entangled in his waistcoat. A startled teller looked down at Billy and said in a curious tone: 'Excuse me, is this a hold-up?' Billy replied: 'No, mate, it's a cock-up.'

For that attempt Billy received a three-year sentence, and when his wife came to visit him in hospital, he told her to bake a cake and put a file in it, as he was determined to escape.

His wife said: 'The file's no problem, Billy, but how the hell do you bake a cake?' She was a rotten cook, in fact Fanny Cradock used to picket her oven. Anyway, she did the cake and duly delivered it to Billy. On her next visit, Billy told her: 'Get me a power saw, a drill and some dynamite.' She said: 'Isn't the file any good that I put in the cake?' Billy shook his head: 'I don't know, love, I can't break the bloody cake open.'

Fred Enterprise is the keynote to a Lancastrian's character. On the edge of the Pennines is a small mill town called Milnrow, where the amazing story of Fred Postlewaithe is still recounted.

Fred couldn't read or write, and the only job he could hold down was that of bagging manure in the yard of a brewery that used horse-drawn drays. New management took the distillery over and when it was discovered that Fred couldn't read or write, he was sacked on the spot. On his way home, he called into a small café for a cup of tea. The woman who served him was crying. 'What's up lass?' said Fred. 'Eeh 'eck,' the woman replied. 'My husband dropped dead in the garden this morning whilst he was plucking a cabbage for dinner.' Fred said simply: 'Well I'm blowed, what did you do?' The woman blew her nose and said: 'I opened a tin of peas.'

The upshot was that Fred and the woman got married. They opened a chain of cafés and before long they'd added four fancy restaurants, a bakery and six frozen-food stores to their varied collection. Within five years they were multi-millionaires with a grand house that overlooked Hollingworth Lake, and that's posh for you.

Fred's story reached the television companies, and Fred was soon the subject of the programme *This Is Your Life*. Eamonn Andrews sat Fred down in the studio of Thames Television and the show began. Men and women came on to pay tribute to Fred's rise to fame in the catering trade, and it was, in parts, a very moving account of a poor boy made good.

Finally, Eamonn Andrews gave Fred the *This Is Your Life* book, and he said with sincerity: 'Fred Postlewaithe, you can't read or write, yet you've accomplished all this. If you could have done so, what might you have been doing today?' Fred grinned, and said softly: 'Bagging horse shit.'

ON LANCASHIRE WOMEN

Martha It may sound like sheer parochial affectation, but in my considered opinion Lancashire women are the prettiest in the country. Apart from my wife, that is. Don't get me wrong, I'm not saying she's that ugly, but when she sucks a lemon, the lemon pulls a face. For all that, my wife does possess many things that I know some men admire . . . like muscles and a duelling scar.

Long before I was forcibly dragged to the altar, I courted a sweet lass called Martha who hailed from Ramsbottom, which lies up the A56 from Bury. Ours was a tragic affair. I remember we used to hold hands on the bus; it took some doing, I was upstairs and she was down. One balmy evening I took her to a spirited little French restaurant in Blackburn. The menu was all in French so I ordered *Polet avec frit du pom.* The waiter said: 'You can't have that.' I said: 'Why not?' He replied: 'That's the band.' I recall that we danced a Hungarian polka, which surprised everybody else because the band was playing the Last Waltz. Martha was a big girl; we'd been dancing for ten minutes before I realized she was still sitting down.

By the light of the guttering candle on the table between us, I could tell that she was emotionally moved when I told her that I loved her very dearly. I reached across the table to kiss her lips, and she snatched her head away angrily and I fell on the candle. It took the head waiter fifteen minutes to get the wick from up my nose.

Afterwards we walked back to her home, and she whispered that she was going to slip into something cool. An hour later I found her sitting in the fridge. Then it happened, that thousand-to-one quirk of fate that led to tragedy. Martha fell asleep on her water bed, the house caught fire and she was poached to death. I've never forgotten her, and I often return to Ramsbottom and sit in the rock garden where we got stoned together.

Florence Potts She escaped from Yorkshire during the dumpling riots in Leeds, and she settled in a posh suburb of Manchester called

Didsbury – so posh that when people there ate fish, they wore a yachting cap. In Didsbury, all the cats' cinder boxes were split-level and they always had grapes on the table even if nobody was ill.

Florence married a clown from Burnley and made a fortune knitting freckles for a joke shop. Her chief claim to fame was finding out that prawns with short legs went deaf very quickly.

Cissie Plumm Cissie hailed from Bacup, high above Rochdale. She is still remembered for her fight to save the Horned Whelk, in Morecambe Bay. Because of man's relentless search for natural gas, silt became disturbed on the ocean bed, and for the whelk which relies on eyesight to find a mate, problems arose. A beachcomber found that half-blinded whelks were trying to mount discarded ice cream cartons at Grange-over-Sands, and in Fleetwood whelks were using shrimps in gang bangs.

Before long it became apparent that the ecological balance was threatened. Because the Horned Whelk had no nose, it couldn't be fitted with National Health glasses, and nobody knew what to do until Cissie invented small wing mirrors that could be riveted to the ears of the whelk, thus giving the male of the species a chance to get at it, as it were. Today, the Horned Whelk can enjoy life to the full: Cissie organizes coach trips for them, and they go to the Lake District to see Kendal Morris Dancers; on the way home, they sing to an accordion and whistle at tins of salmon in the shops. Cissie Plumm was to be given a medal as a tribute from the French Army but they couldn't find a general who would kiss her.

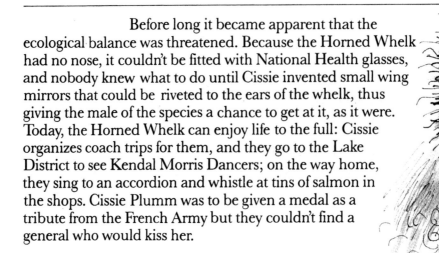

Harriet Wrench She trained as an opera singer in Venice but had to leave because of wet feet. For years she sang in the Royal Opera House, Leigh, and her rendering of 'Oh For The Wings Of A Dove' once shattered a midwife's windscreen three miles away.

Her husband, Alf, was a very thin man; his job was to clean out clarinets from the inside, and he had money tied up in the hem of his singlet.

Harriet's distinguished career began to fade when she started to imagine that she was Prince Philip and wanted to play polo round the council flats. Harriet made just one record: it was put together from old carpet tufts, which she thought was the only way she'd make a pile. Today she lives quietly in the lovely village of Langho which is on the way to Whalley on the A666. She breeds bulldogs, which amazes some people because bulldogs normally do it themselves.

Amy Sprockett Amy was born in Barnoldswick of mixed parents: her father was a man and her mother was a woman. Amy went bald in a

box of apricots and never married. She didn't do a lot until she was fifty-three, but she looked taller.

She opened a shop in Gisburn, selling meat pies and sausage rolls, and one day discovered that she could teach pies to yodel in hot milk. People flocked from near and far to watch her talk to her pies and to hear them sing Alpine laments in a bucket. When she died, the good folk of Gisburn made sure that everybody would look up to Amy . . . they buried her in a tree.

Ethel Codd Lancashire's only Olympic underwater swimmer. Ethel was a big lass, in fact she got her knickers on prescription. They certainly were large garments, those drawers; she didn't have elastic in them, she used Swish Rail. Every time she hung her nightdress out on the line to dry, a family of gypsies used to move in. She was last seen in the public baths in Radcliffe, a dozy little town outside Bury, lying on the bottom at the deep end. Her husband was intensely proud of her. He said to the baths attendant: 'Isn't it amazing how she can hold her breath for so long?' The attendant snorted and replied scornfully: 'She's nowt but a show-off, her.' Ethel Codd's husband was justifiably annoyed. 'What do you mean, she's a show-off?' he bellowed. The attendant replied: 'She's been down there a month.'

The Lancashire Witches And Rex Surely, even those poor souls who live in Catford must have heard about the ill-famed Lancashire witches. History drips with stories of the satanic lasses who practised the Black Arts. Even in this enlightened day and age, God-fearing folk who live in Downham village and Chatburn will tell you that they never venture up Pendle Hill – the Mound of Evil, some people still call it. Dark Pendle of legend . . . in summer, the sun never shines on that grim heap; I know, for many is the time I have driven past its frowning shadow. At night, the hill seems to come alive and throb with some deep energy. High up there, near Ogden Reservoir, lived the witch of witches, a creature whose name made the strongest men shudder . . .

Doris Ramsden It is said that Doris once swallowed a live pig, and when she burped, she knocked down a Wimpey bungalow. Small and hunched, she lived in a tumbledown cottage in Barley. A brave priest once tried to grapple with Doris; she threw disinfectant over his cassock and was heavily fined for a bleach of the priest. She could cure warts by rubbing them with a bat's liver dipped in cocoa, and on one occasion she stopped onions growing by coaxing a stoat to break wind on them. Doris vanished one night when the moon rode across the heavens like a waxen chariot, and she left behind her faithful dog, Rex.

The dog was seized by drunken louts from the Fox and Grapes who stoned it to death; its tail was cut off and put behind the bar in the lounge of the pub. On Walpurgis Eve, when demons

abound, there was a knock at midnight on the door of the Fox and Grapes. The landlord, one Sam Hardcastle, a burly no-nonsense type, gingerly opened the door and there stood the ghost of Rex. Sam staggered back as the shimmering spirit of the canine wavered in front of his eyes, which by this time were like two chapel hat pegs, and he stuttered: 'Eeeh, Rex, what the 'ell do thee want? I never did you any harm, why hast thee cum to haunt me?'

Rex stood on his hind legs and to Sam's astonishment spoke: 'Sam Hardcastle, I am the spirit of Rex the dog who had his tail cut off. I cannot enter the other world until I am a complete ghost again. Help me, Sam, give me my tail back and I shall never come back to haunt you again.' Sam recovered his composure, took a snuffbox out of his waistcoat and snuffled a pinch up his broad nostrils. 'I'd like to help you, Rex,' he said sombrely. 'But, as you can see, it's midnight.' The dog looked at him and moaned: 'What's that got to do with it?' Sam said: 'Well, it's too late to re-tail spirits at this hour.'

PART THREE

MADE
IN
LANCASHIRE

THE SPIRIT OF INDUSTRY

The world is fully aware of Lancashire's contribution to industry: our cotton mills, our coalfields, the giant engineering plants in Trafford Park; our great history of shipbuilding at Barrow-in-Furness. There is a superabundance of documentary and physical evidence testifying to Lancashire's importance in both the Industrial Revolution and in modern technology. What the world may be unaware of, however, is that Lancashire bristles with other sorts of industries. For instance, in a remote part of Bowland is the world's biggest pot gnome factory.

For years, this factory has turned out glazed pelicans and clay-fired elves for every garden in Europe. From all over the planet, midgets used to come and model for pot pixies and gnomes that would one day grace a fishpond in Dulwich.

Things were going well until three Dutch dwarfs decided to form a union; overnight, there was trouble. Midgets complained that they were getting cramp by sitting for hours with a fishing rod, and they demanded free sandwiches and shorter steps on buses. In 1965 a strike was called, and picket lines stopped non-union midgets from going in to work. The militant little men started walking under their foreman's legs and tying fireworks to his suspenders. This led to sabotage in the tin duck section and somebody melted a plastic hen to a pit fairy's foot. Exports dropped after a glazed flamingo was dropped on a docker's stepson, and six boxes of clay imps were smeared with Marmite.

Police were called in when a dwarf who'd had a Guinness wrote on the back of a widow's handbag that Snow White was really a pouf. Today, the factory is deserted and the Japanese have cornered the market in pot gnomes, which also take photographs by remote control when dipped in paraffin.

Farnworth Shoots Ahead Farnworth, a small town near Bolton, was the first site of a plant that produced a fuel substitute for petrol. It was a secret mixture of turtle manure and squirrel sweat, and it was claimed by the manufacturers that the average car could do two hundred miles to the gallon on it.

In tests carried out, a Morris Minor saloon was fitted with an eight-ton boiler on the roof and a gas turbo engine fixed on the rear bumpers. Assorted turtles were allowed to swim in prune juice and, instead of a fan belt, a squirrel was placed in front of the radiator with a set of pedals. A carrot was left to swing inside the engine and as the squirrel made a dart for it, the creature had no choice but to pedal. This created a draught which went up some pipes to where the turtles were, and the draught made their eyes water so much they ducked under the prune juice and found themselves drinking the stuff, which after an hour created internal problems. After evacuation had taken place the squirrel, now sweating heavily, wiped its brow, and the moisture blended with the gas from the dung deposit causing a spark to jump across the starting plugs, and lo! the car moved.

It was, however, impractical. The turtles couldn't be trusted and the squirrels developed tennis elbow after the first ten thousand miles. It was a bold experiment and deserved a better fate.

Exploding Toenails It was to Oldham that many eyes turned when a factory opened up there in the late Sixties with the intention of manufacturing self-destruct paper socks. In principle the idea was a good one: when a man had worn the socks for more than two days, they would blow up and the wearer would have to buy a new pair. Alas, the built-in charge was often too intense, and several men had toenails that exploded and caused panic at tea dances.

But at least Lancashire does look to the future, which is more than can be said for, say, Lincolnshire; or would you rather be a mule?

Nobel Prize We in Lancashire are proud of our agricultural progress. Our county, as I have previously mentioned, is one of the largest dairy producers in the world, and we have men who are constantly experimenting with new ideas that will one day elevate mankind to a higher standard of living. As the population of this planet increases, the supply of food will become an ever-greater problem, and so Lancashire's agricultural experimentation is an expanding industry. Seth Hardbotham at his farm in Slaidburn will one day, in my considered opinion, win a Nobel Prize for his efforts. Only last year this remarkable man crossed a giraffe with a pig and produced a seven-foot pork chop. He crossed a hen with a parrot and the result was an egg that not only boiled quicker, it told you when it was done. He really is an amazing man, and his latest effort, although a failure, certainly made the headlines.

Seth crossbred a kangaroo with a turkey. The idea was to produce a bird for Christmas that could be stuffed on the outside. It didn't work, all he got was an egg that looked like a boomerang and kept punching the bacon.

Saviour Of The Eskimos Over in Gisburn, that most agreeable of hamlets, is a man who has done more than anyone to protect the Eskimo from becoming an extinct people. How, you might well ask, did a Lancastrian achieve this? The man, Alf Potter, grew peas for a living and one day, whilst taking his children round a zoo, he took his handkerchief from his pocket and some of his home-grown peas fell out and went into an enclosure which was a pen for polar bears. Instantly, the bears lumbered over and ate the peas with relish and a carton of whipped cream.

That night on television, there was a programme showing the plight of the Eskimo in his search for meat. Alf knew he had the answer, and within the month he was swaddled in furs in Greenland.

His idea was simplicity in itself. He cut a hole in the ice floe then scattered his peas around the hole. When a polar bear came down for a pea, Alf kicked it in the ice hole.

I am proud of such men.

LA MODE

For centuries, people in other parts of the British Isles thought that Lancashire women wore nowt but clogs and shawls and capacious bloomers under a stiff calico shift, and that the menfolk went to bed in a scarf over a shirt with no collar, a flat coarse felt cap, steel-tipped boots and baggy corduroy pants. That, of course, is quite ridiculous; they took their trousers off before they went to bed.

To a certain extent, however, that image was true. It was created in the grime-stacked clouds hovering above belching factories, and in the poverty endured. But remember this well, it was Lancashire that made Britain rich. Others warmed their backsides on the coal wrenched from Lancashire pits, and London society wore the cotton that Lancashire folk toiled in damp dark places to produce.

It's nice to know that things are changing rapidly now. The world hums the songs the Beatles sang, and young fashion designers in Lancashire are leading the way for all the Bright Young Things.

From Westhaughton comes more good news of daring beachwear created by 'Bo-Bo' Wimpey. He recently unveiled his collection to a hushed assembly in Manchester's Free Trade Hall. First, we saw his quite mad yet adorable copper-tipped bikini in bright puce with a tin-embroidered hem peeping from an iron gusset. After that came his divine two-piece backless off-the-hip self-draining swimsuit that gives a whole new meaning to pigeon chests. As an extra, there is a towelling robe in flounced leather with slate pegs and charcoal antlers.

For my money, though, his spring collection last year really made the international scene with a bang. There he showed us:

1 A trailing gown with a handkerchief hem, which set off in fine style the steamed creased organdie strapless donkey jacket in burnt sienna with hip-length gaiters.

2 A string vest with rubber side panels and a pleated nose rope – a harmony when worn with see-through weighted socks and a red carnival hat incorporating blue serge earmuffs.

The famous hair stylist 'Cuddles' Gaylord actually came from St Helen's. I thought that would shake you, but it's true!

He stunned the orbit of the débutante with his 'Bald' look for long women. The hair is scrubbed off one side of the head and then panel pins are welded to the scalp, and hot mincemeat is blown over them. Down the other side of the cranium, the hair is cropped and burnt with joss sticks and a mouse is sewn in by the ankle and fastened to the neck. The whole effect is one of allure, especially when a wine rack is screwed on.

The Stage Suit The garment and barnet industries were less volatile when I first began to be noticed in show business, and someone advised me to purchase a really top-class stage suit. I was given the address of a tailor who had premises in Salford, which is Manchester's twin across the muddy Irwell.

When I got there, the shop wasn't what I had expected at all. I perceived a dimly lit, grubby room with fly-blown windows that overlooked a narrow seedy alleyway. The name above the shop had been transformed by vandals or a dissatisfied customer into a rather vulgar saying, which I refuse to print here. I entered, and a small Jewish gentleman with a tape measure around his shoulders minced across to me and said: 'Oy vay, a physique you have mah bhoy. Such a suit on you would make my reputation already.' So saying, he held up a three-piece suit that looked as if it had been made for Quasimodo. I shook my head, told him that I was in show business and what my needs were. He nodded gravely and then went on in a torrent of words:

'For you I make a suit . . . cost you three hundred pounds, the best only for you.' Three hundred pounds in 1962 was a hell of a lot of lucre and I about-turned smartly. In a flash he was between me and the door. 'Wanna know what you get for that kind of money? Well, I tell you. The wool for the suit grows only on the belly of a very rare Himalayan goat that jumps from mountain top to mountain top. To get the wool I hire a team of Tasmanian acrobats who form a pyramid in a gully, and then when the goat leaps across, the one on the top jumps up and plucks handfuls of wool. Next the thread to fasten the material together comes from the sinews of the Baltic Eel, and to get these sinews, we employ a special diving team who plunge into the waters and obtain the sinews needed. Only from the knee we take them, so it's a lengthy process. Next, we send a photograph of you in the nude to a famous sculptor in Rome who does a life-size statue of you, so that every curve and muscle is faithfully recorded. Now the wool and the sinews are sent to a secret place, ready to be made up. But we have to have the right sort of buttons for it, and we use the inner shell of the Polynesian Hermit Crab; not many about at this time of the year, but we manage. All that's left then is for the suit to be run up, as we say in the trade, and you will be the smartest man on the stage ever.'

After he had finished his curious narrative, I said to him grudgingly: 'Well, it certainly sounds marvellous. If I order one, how long will it be before I can have it?' He lit a battered cigar butt and replied: 'Tomorrow?'

FIGHTING MEN

In every city, in every town, in every village of
Lancashire you will see memorial stones
commemorating the sacrifice that Lancashire
men gave in the slaughter of World War One. The
Lancashire Fusiliers earned seven VCs before
breakfast during that most dreadful of conflicts, and
the diminutive Manchester Bantams faced the Prussian
Guards on the Somme. Kendal men died to a man almost
in 1917, and for years after, Kendal was known as the Town
of Widows.

World War Two gave Lancashire its chance to
produce the great aircraft that would eventually crush the enemy into
defeat. At Chadderton, the Avro factory made the Lancaster, most
famous bomber of them all, and De Havilland in the east of the
county made the versatile Mosquito. Even today, in Preston, the
European MRCA fighter is in full production. In Lancashire also
were munitions factories, and mills that made the parachutes, the
uniforms, the bandages and the survival packs. The mournful sound
of the factory siren would herald the advance of the Lancashire
women in their shawls and clogs, spilling out from sooty homes
towards the vast industrial expanses of Lancashire at war. They
trained the Air Force at Kirkham near Blackpool, and made a damn
good job of it.

As a small boy, I watched the
Territorials go through their paces in
Broadhurst Park, and I thrilled to the sight of
fighters soaring into the torn skies from the base
at Bowdon.

I myself, I might modestly add, come from a
military family. You've heard of the Thin Red Line? My family were
the Fat Yellow Streak. My great-great-great-grandfather fought with
Wellington; they couldn't trust him with a gun. Legend has it, that
whilst running away from Waterloo he was peppered with so many
cannonballs, they didn't bury him, he was weighed in for scrap.
During World War One, my grandfather had so many white feathers

sent to him, he played the Oldham Empire for four years as Mother Goose. Perhaps the finest coward in the Dawson family, though, was my father. He once cancelled a holiday in Jersey because he had heard about the Battle of the Flowers. What a character: he was at Dunkirk when the first shot was fired, he was under a bed in Bolton when the second one went off.

I served in The Queen's Bays, Second Dragoon Guards for my National Service, and I was asked if I would like a commission. I said no, thank you, I'd prefer a straight salary. There is in fact only one blot on my brief military career. I found great difficulty in getting out of bed in the morning, and I was court-martialled for the offence of being a sluggard. The Commanding Officer said to me very sternly: 'Now look here, Dawson, don't you hear the bugle play in the mornings?' I said piteously: 'No, sir, they always play it while I'm asleep.'

Lavender Over Germany But, thank heaven above, Lancashire has had its fair share of heroes. I'd like to tell a story about one. His name was Julian Aspinall and he was, well, not exactly masculine if you see what I'm driving at. Let's put it this way, at school his nickname was 'Lavender'.

Much to everybody's amazement, on the outbreak of war in 1939 Julian joined the Royal Air Force and became a first-class pilot. He caused quite a sensation when he first arrived at Bowlee Camp, near Middleton: he had frills on his parachute and he carried a mauve gas-mask case. His Wing Commander was horrified, especially after Julian's first encounter in the air during the Battle Of Britain. When he landed, Julian was asked by an enterprising journalist: 'I say, old man, what was it like up there with all those bullets flying about?' Julian sighed, ran his fingers through his curly blond locks, pouted, and said breathlessly: 'Oh, the noise, the people.'

Slowly, Britain won the war in the air, and things became a little easier. In spring 1944, the Bowlee Air Base was given its last assignment – to drop leaflets over Germany urging the enemy to surrender. Six Spitfires set out to do the job, and 'Lavender' Aspinall led the group over the North Sea.

That night, only five of the fighters returned; 'Lavender' was missing. All through the night they kept watch for his aircraft, but to no avail, and a mantle of gloom settled over Bowlee.

In the mess, silence hung like a curtain of reproach as his comrades sank into their thoughts. 'Confound it,' spoke his Wing Commander. 'I miss the old pouf, I must say.' The rest of the airmen nodded in agreement and several burst into tears. 'It doesn't seem right, not seeing his garter belt hanging in his locker,' said one man. Another nodded and remarked: 'I miss the scent of his perfume and the way he laughed when he danced.' 'Lavender' did not return; soon the war was over, the camp was dispersed, and the men returned to civilian life.

In 1958 the Wing Commander, now retired, went back to Bowlee to revisit the scene of his wartime posting. He lit up his pipe, and limped onto the derelict runway, and stood there with a hostile wind cuffing his features as he lost himself in a welter of old memories. Just then, the noise of an aeroplane could be heard droning overhead. Startled, the Wing Commander looked up, and then fell back in astonishment, for coming in to land was a Spitfire.

As the aircraft taxied to a halt, the retired Wing Commander stumped over to it, and nearly swooned when he saw none other than 'Lavender' Aspinall jump out, looking exactly as he had done in 1944. 'Hello, Wingey, old fruit,' simpered 'Lavender.' 'Hope I'm not late, ducky?' His old commander gasped. 'Late? You idiot, the war's been over for bloody years, where the hell have you been? You only went to drop leaflets over Germany.' Julian 'Lavender' Aspinall clasped his hands to his chest and said in a ringing tone of despair: 'Drop the leaflets, did you say? I've been round putting them through the letter-boxes.'

Typical Lancashire devotion to duty, wouldn't you say? Our county abounds with such tales.

LES TRIPES LANCASTRIENNES

Nowhere in Britain will you find the range of foods that are so readily available in Lancashire. Tripe, cowheel, trotters, pressed veal, brawn, muffins, black puddings – all of these are non-existent in, say, impoverished London. Nay, you haven't lived until you've sampled a Chorley Flat Cake or an Eccles Cake, and who can fully describe the joy of sinking the teeth into a chip butty?

Just what do we have in Lancashire that can whip the taste buds into a rhapsodic state? Well, you could do worse than get these down you for a start:

Lancashire Hot Pot A mouth-watering dish indeed, and it cannot be rivalled. For it you need at least a pound of lean skirt from a good butcher. The skirt is chopped into lumps and you bung it in a pan with diced potatoes and carrots and onions with herbs and seasoning and anything else that may take your fancy, although marmalade doesn't go too well with it. Shove the lot into a casserole dish with good honest soft Lancashire water culled from Thirlemere, and let it do on a low light. Add a giant suet crust and get stuck in lad, and to hell with your girth.

Black Pudding Nowt like 'em. Big, black and beautiful, they lie on the plate like sensuous Nubians and beckon the unwary. The thing they fail to do in the South, is boil the damn things. *Never* fry them. Boil them for about twenty minutes, slice down the middle and add black pepper and Alps of butter and become primeval. In previous chapters I have extolled the virtues of this magnificent obelisk and I still do. Lie back in an easy chair after two have been dispatched into the tum, and listen to the grunts of approval from within the disgestive tract.

Beware, however, of imitations. There is only one Black Pudding worthy enough to stumble down the gullet, and that is the one created in Bury. Those sinister Yorkists make them, but with malice in their black hearts.

Tripe Salivant, savoury, good to look at and good to eat ... that is tripe. Boil it, stew it, eat it raw with vinegar and it'll put five years on your life and hairs on your chest. Many firmly believe it does the sex life the power of good and others swear that it can straighten round shoulders. With onions it is a dish to make you slaver idiotically, and I've known people who have been prepared to kill with their bare hands for a plateful of celebrated Black Tripe. Did you know that the French eat as much, if not more, tripe than we do in this country? Of course they have to ruin it with their customary zeal by doing tripe as a flambé. No, tripe must be faced with courage and one must grab a trembling sheet of it with aplomb.

Chip Butty Spread at least four layers of best butter on a thick slice of fresh bread, then add a heap of hot greasy chips, press another slice of well-buttered bread on top, and dig in. Swill down with a mash of fine tea brewed in a copper kettle, and keep away from 'Speak Your Weight' machines.

Cowheel Ram it in a stew and watch it thicken the gravy into a monolithic slab of superb jelly that will make you drool with pleasure. Cowheel keeps the 'flu at bay, and it has been known to cure advanced cases of croup.

Liverpool Scouse Basically, it's very much like a Lancashire Hot Pot, but things are added which perforce must remain a mystery for all time. It's piping hot, fat-inducing, lovely to look at, and delightful to know. With Scouse, anything goes in it, sometimes a drunken lodger or an unwelcome aunt. It takes years to train for its consumption, but once that is achieved – probably with the help of a guru – you can't face anything else.

We also have vast quantities of pressed meats and cooked meats, pies and brawn, that go hand in hand with pig's trotters and Barm Cakes or muffins and, for me, there is nothing to match a Haslingden Crumpet.

What's that you cry? You like fish? Well, Lancashire is definitely for you. From Fleetwood you can get clams and kippers and cod and plaice in great fettle. St Anne's-on-Sea will give you the finest shrimps you've ever tackled without a safety net. There are trout and salmon streams inland that can give Scotland a ten break (as we say up 'ere). Some of our canals are being farmed for crayfish, and reet tasty they are too.

No, you have no excuse for not coming to see our county. We have it all. Once you're here, we'll let you go and fish for the Morecambe Shark, a fearsome creature with no teeth but, by God, if it catches you it'll give thee a nasty suck. Many people have tried to catch one, but it only rises to the surface when it breaks wind at Easter. One old timer hit a Morecambe Shark with his sandal when it tried to chew his toffee pig. It rolled over on its side and his wife, who was eating ribs and cabbage from a parcel, found that her corsets were alive with whitebait. The Loch Ness Monster has nowt on the Morecambe Shark, and it loves curried eggs.

The Lancashire Gourmet One lunch time, a little man wearing a flat cap and carrying a whippet walked into the Savoy Hotel and sat himself down in the dining room. The head waiter paled when he saw the ill-garbed fellow blow his nose on a napkin and he stormed across and ordered the man out. 'Look 'ere lad,' said our hero. 'If thy

try to get rid of me, I will cause such a bloody row, tha'll wonder what's hit thee. I come from Bolton, an' my money's as good as anybody's.'

Reluctantly, the head waiter gave orders to serve him and get him out as soon as possible. Suddenly, the little man shouted: 'Ere, I can't eat this soup.' This was too much for the head-waiter and he grabbed the man by his shoulders and spun him round on his chair. 'How dare you say that you cannot eat our soup, you product of an industrial wasteland. In all the years that I have been at the Savoy, I have never had to endure such crass ignorance as confronts me now. You walk in here, you Northern clod, with that disgusting animal, and you have the gall to rant in your flat-toned coarse voice that you cannot eat our soup . . . The Savoy is the Valhalla for all discerning gourmets. Crowned heads of Europe have waxed eulogies over our quail in aspic, to name but one of our superior dishes. Only last week, that fine actress Elizabeth Taylor drooled over the liver pâté. Prince Charles himself speaks most highly of the quality of the Savoy rib of beef that is to be found on the groaning table. From all over the world, you despicable urchin, letters of thanks are received every day, adoring letters from satisfied lovers of *haute cuisine*, and you, you dreadful little Lancashire lout, have the audacity to say that you cannot eat the soup. Now, before I pitch you out into the gutters from whence you no doubt sprang, I will ask you, why can't you eat the soup?' The little man lit a Woodbine and said: 'I haven't got a spoon.'

ART SUBLIME

In the art world, Lancashire has become a major centre thanks to a pre-war Russian sex symbol called Hildegarde Crumm. She came to Manchester to appear in *Coronation Street* which, naturally, is filmed in Manchester. And where's Manchester? Why, Lancashire of course. Do you see what I'm driving at?

Hildegarde was signed up to play the part of a tug-boat captain with a bad heart who falls in love with a machinist. She liked the North so much she sat on a canvas in her suede knickers; the imprint she made was coloured in with Dulux paint, and it was sold as *Mood Over A Urinal*. Since that first painting, she has sold over a hundred originals and her knickers are valued at two hundred thousand pounds, without elastic.

Lancashire produced one of the finest writers the world has ever known. You won't have heard of him because he had no sense of direction and he was pretty lousy at geography. His name was Wimberry Hotteroyd and he hailed from Blackpool. He wrote three great novels and never made it – and all because of his lack of direction.

One was called *All Quiet On The Eastern Front*. This was followed three years later with *West Of Eden,* after which he wrote *North Pacific*. It was a tremendous tragedy and his mother blamed herself for keeping him off school with measles. She brooded all her life and put knots in his braces.

Wimberry is not alone in his setbacks. Another man, a songwriter, suffered the ignominy of failure because he was colour-blind. I refer naturally enough to Claude Barraclough, who wrote such numbers as 'Blue Sails In The Sunset'. Do you remember 'I Want Some Green Roses For A Red Lady?' A favourite amongst teenagers was his 'Grey Sports Coat And A Black Carnation'. It was a great shame indeed, and at the early age of forty-four Claude went mad playing snooker.

My own flirtation with high culture began at a tender age. When I was a small lad living in the mean streets of Manchester's Collyhurst district, my mother was determined that I should become a great musician. She bought me a second-hand violin, and dutifully I attended music lessons given by an old alcoholic musician whose chief claim to fame was that he had been fired by Geraldo.

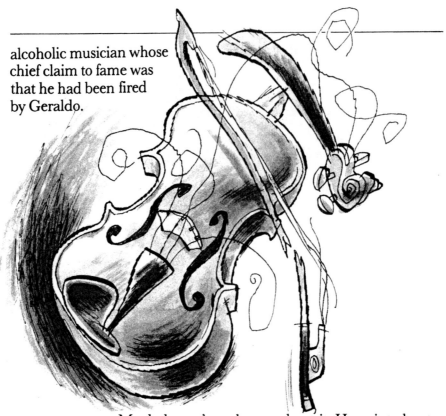

    My dad wasn't too happy about it. He pointed out forcibly that our neighbours, a rough lot to say the least, might not take kindly to an urchin scratching on such an instrument, so I'd better not play the thing in the streets. Being only a youngster, I didn't listen, and one night I came home with the violin wrapped around my neck. My mother slumped on our one decent chair and burst into tears. 'How could anybody do such a thing?' she sobbed. 'What a terrible thing to do to a little lad.' I whimpered back: 'That's nothing, Mum, wait till you see where they've put the bow.'

    My father bent me down and had a look. 'Thank God he wasn't learning the clarinet,' he told mother.

A Genius Called Alfred It was in a small house in Oldham that a child prodigy was born. His name, Alfred Sidebottom; the year, 1921. His father was a dour man with faulty dentures, but he was the first to recognize his offspring's genius when his son, at the tender age of three, played Beethoven's Fifth Symphony upon a battered piano. 'Eeh, bloody hell,' said his dad, and dropped his dominoes.

    By the time Alf was eleven, the world of music was

at his feet. Moscow, New York, Sydney, he appeared everywhere – Alf, the greatest exponent of Beethoven, Wagner and Ravel ever to grace the major concert halls. As he toured the world, people began to notice that every time the lad walked on to a stage to perform, he carried a piece of paper in his hand; before long, there was wild speculation about the contents of the paper. Many learned men vouchsafed that Alfred had been given it as a gift from God Himself, others maintained that the paper was the key to his genius, and on it must be written the secret of the lad's greatness. Alf went on from success to success, always with his bit of paper clenched in his hand. As his father put it: 'Eeh, bloody hell.' Envious musicians hired burglars to try to steal the paper from the lad's grasp as he slept, but to no avail. Meanwhile the rumours grew. At the age of fifteen, Alf Sidebottom became the North's greatest living composer and his fame spread even to Outer Mongolia, where he gave a series of concerts in a pigskin tent. The boy was becoming exhausted by all the travelling and adulation heaped upon him, and he fell ill in Africa. His father was very worried and said: 'Eeh, bloody hell.' Doctors fought to save the sinking Alf, but at the early age of seventeen, he died, still clutching the piece of paper in his chubby fist.

His funeral was attended by every head of state in the world and his father said: 'Eeh, bloody hell.' Two years after his son's demise, the courts decided that the piece of paper, which now lay in a bank vault, should be taken out and given to the world of music for the benefit of all aspiring musicians. Solemnly, chosen dignitaries assembled, and millions of people waited with bated breath for them to read what was on the paper that Alf always looked at before he conducted a symphony orchestra. At long last the secret would be out in the open, and his father said: 'Eeh, bloody hell.'

Slowly the piece of creased paper was unfolded, and there it was: Alfred Sidebottom's guide to genius, the reason for his true greatness:

PIANO   DRUMS

ME

Isn't that a moving story? What do you mean, it's a load of tripe?

SPORTING HISTORY

There is only one place to see cricket at its finest: Old Trafford, Manchester. There, in the hallowed sanctum, Australia crashed into dust, never mind ashes. 'Twas there that I saw Yorkshire, that shifty county, collapse like a set of badly planed dominoes atop the sacred turf.

You say you are a football fan? Take your pick from the greatest teams that ever pulled on a jock strap: Everton, Liverpool, Manchester City, Manchester United, Blackburn, Bolton, Preston . . . yes, verily, even Blackpool; although, these days, to watch Blackpool is about as interesting as changing sheets in a bed-wetting clinic. What a team! One Saturday, the referee announced the crowd changes. There's also Oldham Athletic and Bury, great for laughs.

Now we come to Rugby League. Wigan, Leigh, Swinton, St Helen's . . . aye, and Warrington and Runcorn before they messed about with county boundaries. For the upper-class hooligan, there is always Rugby Union: St Anne's, Rossall, Salford, to name but a few. Eeh, when those lads bend down in't scrum . . .

In St Anne's you can watch, or participate in, sand yachting and crown bowling. Go no further for golf than the Fylde Coast: Fairhaven, Royal Lytham, Green Drive, Old Links, Knott End, Fleetwood, and if you go the other way there is Birkdale and Penwortham and Preston. Top-class tennis is played at Didsbury in Manchester. It's all there, you see.

I come from a sporting family: my father was a boxer and my mother was a cocker spaniel. My grandfather used to putt the shot, until they saw where he was putting it, and my uncle was a pole vaulter, but the Pole got fed up with it and went home.

But what of the *traditional* Lancashire sports, once so flourishing? Many, alas, have vanished with the passage of time. Let us hasten to note down a few of them, before it is too late.

Lancaster Soot Juggling Last seen in a caravan that was lying on its side. Two teams of midgets, nude except for their socks, juggled with loose soot until one of them had a breakdown. The record was held by Arthur, a dwarf who had a hammer toe until his wife made him wear a trilby in cold weather.

Oswaldtwistle Head Banging Played by sixteen men and a child bride, this sport was very popular in the early Thirties. It was a complicated game in which each player banged his head against a brick wall until his feet ached. Anyone who said he had a headache was made to stand in ox manure and his rent was paid for a week.

Kirkham Buttock Jousting Played by the Vikings when it was foggy, this game never really took on in popularity. Briefly, three men and a goose bent down on hot grass and tried to shove the goose up an opponent's vest. You had to keep your back to a brewery and count to ten with your nose in a bucket of dried mice.

Chadderton Gravy Racing This sport was banned at the turn of the century after a spinster with a bad leg found traces of Bisto in her hand-painted drawers. Three hundred men usually took part in the race, each one carrying a handful of warm gravy balanced on a rubber hat; the object was to run backwards to a special hole that was raised four feet above the ground. The winner received a bag of rabbits and a free truss for any charity of his choice.

Longridge Horse Blowing Lots of money used to be wagered on this most peculiar of sports, and in some cases, men went bald. The idea was to lift up a horse's tail, and with the aid of a hollow stick blow into the animal's anus and then jump up and down on a damp balloon whilst chewing a magpie's ankle. Tragedy struck in 1907 when Squire Henry forgot to take his pipe out of his mouth when he blew and he set fire to an elderly stallion. The nag kicked his dentures over a nest of tables and the Squire couldn't go to the lavatory.

Accrington Banana Bending This was a comparatively new sport, introduced into Accrington by a limbo dancer who tried to get into toilets for nothing. Basically, one had to flick lentils into a tray of jam and then bend a banana without the aid of a coathanger. To make it more difficult, each player had to steam-iron a poached egg in a pith helmet and tell the time under a rug. It never appealed to me, and there are not many bananas in Accrington, especially when there's a draught up your kilt.

Chorley Pig Throwing Died out in 1932 after a Jesuit lost his trousers in a bag of suet. The rules were very simple: one simply threw a pig across a yard full of spanners, and the first one to smack its head on a wet sponge was ducked in treacle while an orphan played a bugle on his head.

NIGHT LIFE

Lancashire and show business go hand in hand. In the field of humour, Ulverston gave us Stan Laurel, probably one of the greatest clowns that ever lived. His association with Oliver Hardy created the sort of comedy that bridges any so-called generation gap, and lives on after the demise of the two stars.

Liverpool and Manchester provided Arthur Askey, Ted Ray, Ken Dodd and Johnny Hackett. The clubs still rock with laughter when Jackie Hamilton walks on the stage. Jimmy Tarbuck, the celebrated golf bandit, hails from Liverpool, and he's going from strength to strength in his career. Radio churned out Jimmy Clitheroe and Ted Lune, nor must we forget staunch old campaigners such as Ken Platt and Tony Melody who still give pleasure in abundance. Can we ever forget the immortal Robb Wilton? Yes, he was a Lancashire lad too. Norman Evans, for my money the best panto dame in the business, was a son of the Red Rose. Al Read, one of the finest of all radio comedians, came from Lancashire; so did George Formby, and he didn't do so badly for himself. Young Stan Boardman, Mick Miller and Al Robbins – they are the new breed of laughter-makers who are striving for a place in the sun. God help us, even Bernard Manning is a Manchester lad, alongside Colin Crompton. Did anyone mention Les Dawson?

I thought not; still, he does have the odd decent night.

Where To Go When I was a struggling comedian – and the way
things are, my career as an economic grappler may not be over –
Manchester was the centre of night-life entertainment. Within a
seven-mile radius of Piccadilly, you would find something like three
hundred night clubs, not to mention several more that were
disreputable. Unlike so many clubs in London's West End, these
venues were not rip-off joints. For the price you would pay for a pint
in an ordinary pub, you could see all the top stars of the day.

Great characters such as 'Mountain' Bill Benny, the
wrestler, and Jack McCall started the trend for what became known
as 'Sporting Clubs'. Many had been cinemas in their day, and they
were converted into mammoth concert and cabaret rooms which
could, and did, hold up to about two thousand people. They could
offer entertainment at low prices because of their great turn-over in
audiences. All possessed huge stage areas for orchestras and artistes,
with superb lighting and sound equipment, the sort you would
expect to find in any first-class theatre.

For old time's sake, let's recall a few of these niteries
by name: Dino's, The Northern Sporting Club, The Garden Of
Eden, Cabaret Club, The Stork Room, The Stage And Radio, The
Continental, Chez Joey's, The Piccadilly, The Square Wheel, The
Cromford, Devonshire Sporting Club, Ace Of Clubs, Foo Foo La
Mar's, Athenium, The Blonde Hall, Mr Smith's, Playboy Club . . .
and remember, all these clubs were in spitting distance of one
another. The variety of entertainment was limitless: one night there
would be wrestling, another night would be a sort of provincial
'Mardi Gras' followed by international stars.

In the theatre, too, Manchester led the way. In 1908
Mrs Annie Horniman opened the Gaiety and brought the concept of
repertory theatre to the world. Today, many small auditoriums still
flourish. There is the Library Theatre, The Green Room, the Royal
Exchange and the Palace. The Royal Opera House, a truly
magnificent building, is still with us, though alas, at present it is a
bingo venue, but hopes ride high that it will one day revert to its
proper function. Most pubs in the city offer live entertainment, and
for eating out Manchester now ranks with anywhere in Europe for
varied tastes. There are casinos to delight the gambler and the
timeless Ritz is there for the dedicated dancer.

The tourist with courage will want to go down the 'Barbary Coast' in Salford, and see the pubs where sailors and ladies of the night congregate; sitting at tables that are screwed to the floor in case of trouble. I know these places; I used to play the piano in some of them. The customers were so tough, even the women had cauliflower ears.

Liverpool used to be much better than it is now. The town planners did their best to ruin Liverpool but, as I wrote in an earlier chapter, it's the people who make the city what it is. The humour is self-evident, wherever you go. The Empire Theatre is a huge venue – a wonderful place to play in and visit. In my younger days, I played great dates at The Shakespeare Club and The Hanover Restaurant, alongside such artistes as Cleo Laine and the youthful Des O'Connor. Allison's is still going strong, and a right good night is there to be had by all.

Let's also remember the working men's clubs that are a high point in the social life of every Lancashire town. Most of them offer fantastic value for money; well carpeted and comfortable, they have become the new grounds for emerging talent, and that talent is very good indeed. Go in any one, be it in Bolton or Blackburn, Rochdale or Burnley, and you will be staggered at the high quality of amusement on show. In the old days, when I first started out as an entertainer, these clubs had a very different image. Now Matt Monroe and Bob Monkhouse play them – and they will vouch for the high standards.

All of which brings us back to Blackpool; but it will not be ignored. I have sat in the Horseshoe Bar on South Shore and seen the finest revues ever staged outside Las Vegas. And that is no mere flight of fancy. Everything one's heart desires is in Blackpool, and I will leave it at that. Simply go and experience it for yourself.

So now you know. Lancashire night life is the tops. What you may not know is what it used to be like to play the pubs and clubs in some of the cotton towns. It was, in a word, grim. Partly this is the fault of the weather, but in my beloved county we get a lot of rain. We have to have it, otherwise the cotton would be too dry and it would break. The reason why most of the cotton mills were built nestling beneath the bulk of the Pennines is that when the clouds broke up over the hills, the rain fell and created the atmosphere needed for quality fabrics.

Tintwhistle Blues I still shudder at the memory of playing a cotton mill social club in a gloomy place called Tintwhistle. A tall gaunt man with a huge nose criss-crossed with bulging veins introduced me thus: 'We've never 'ad this feller 'ere before, 'e's a comic so 'e reckons, anyroad, give 'im a clap . . . Len Pawson.' I felt affronted by the mistake in my name, and when I got on stage I managed a grin and remarked: 'Well, well, I've got a different name now. Actually it's Les Dawson.' A tired voice mumbled from among the smoke-wreathed crowd: 'Who the bloody hell cares?' I did not get one chuckle from that motley flax-mottled crew. They sat hunched under open fluorescent lamps that made them look sickly, and they never made a sound apart from slurping from pint pots. When I'd finished my act, if you'll excuse the phrase, the Man With The Big

Nose said in a depressed tone: 'Well, that were the paid turn, now for some real entertainment. One of our own, you all know 'im, he lost a leg when a loom crashed . . . 'ere is 'im . . . Bert Trotter, our very own Bing Crosby.' A fat chap with a metallic click from his right lower appendage heaved himself onto the stage, sang 'The Teddy Bear's Picnic' out of tune and brought the place down. I got paid half my fee, which should have been thirty shillings, and was shown the door.

It was a hard school for an aspiring performer, and many died by the wayside. Many is the time I myself felt like throwing my dreams out of the window and becoming a plumber. It was all summed up for me by a conversation I overheard outside a concert room in Mossley. Two men staggered out, and one turned to the other and said: 'Was the comic any good tonight, Alf?' His mate burped and said: 'He was all reet . . . if you like laughing.' What can you do with people like that?

After a performance in Wigan, I was chaired into the street. 'Put me down, lads!' I cried modestly, 'for this is where I catch the bus.' One blubbery man shouted: 'Tha's not going on't bus . . . tha's going in't bloody canal!'

In a grim, fortress-like club in Accrington, I ran foul of the concert secretary. I had just 'died' yet again before a pyramid of drunken clients, and I now stood at the bar with acid glances piercing me between the shoulder blades. 'Thy was bloody awful, son,' the concert secretary said, as he swayed with the tonnage of booze swilling in his gut. 'I'm not paying thee a penny. Op it.'

I was enraged. 'How dare you,' I snarled. 'My material was too good for them out there, it went right over their heads.' He peered at me and croaked: 'Are thee prepared to say that to the committee?' I nodded and off we climbed up some ramshackle stairs and there, in a small reeking room, sat three burly men – the committee. I told them what I'd said to their concert secretary and after I'd finished they conferred with their heads close together.

'I think the comic's got a point about jokes going over their 'eads,' one man said sagely. 'I allus said we'd put the loudspeakers too high up the walls.'

THE BLACKPOOL LANDLADY

I dwelt briefly on these awesome tyrants in an earlier chapter. But they are unique, a mesmerizing wart on the visage of our great county, and as such demand a deeper examination. Take Mrs X, as we shall call her. She was an enormous woman with eyes that could chill the very marrow. Her husband used to keep a photograph of her near his heart when he was in the Army. He reckoned that if her face could stop a clock, it could stop a bullet.

Yet, year after year, the same visitors returned to her dwelling for more punishment and partial malnutrition. If you came in late, you were denied your biscuits and cocoa! She once hit me across the head because hunger had forced me to steal a peach from a dish on the sideboard. When I left her boarding house, I nailed a kipper under her piano. Two months later, I received a letter from her, in which she wrote: 'We know what it is and who did it, but for God's sake tell us where it is!'

A lot of Blackpool boarding houses catered for theatrical people in the days when the resort had more theatres than it does now. They were often spartan but they were, above all, cheap. The ladies who ran them were show-business experts and, in some cases, frustrated performers themselves. I remember one such gorgon, who served the evening meal while tap dancing around the tables dressed in a pair of shorts and a bolero-style jacket. Another one used to sing sea shanties and juggle with the cruet at the same time. She eventually ran off with a third-rate knife-thrower from Barnsley and they finished up in a side-show re-enacting scenes from the murders of Jack the Ripper.

Dry Sherry And Solids Two comedians, who have since become household names, once stayed at Blackpool in a house that was a cross between Lenin's Tomb and an Arab urinal. One of the comedians, who shall remain nameless for a variety of reasons, was quite a wine buff, and he had brought with him a bottle of expensive dry sherry. They shared the same bill at the theatre and looked forward to enjoying a glass or two in the evening after the show.

They got back to the digs only to find that some of the sherry was missing; at least two glassfuls had been poured from the bottle. They were both incensed, and, laying the blame firmly on the landlady, they decided on a drastic course of action: they both peed in the bottle and put the cork back. The ritual went on all week; they'd arrive back, have supper, the sherry was down again and so they would pee in the bottle and recork it. On the last night, the landlady smiled at them and said what a pleasure it had been having them stay with her. Both comics were inwardly squirming with glee, then she said: 'I hope you've enjoyed my cooking, and especially my trifle that you had every night. I hope you didn't mind, by the way, but I used to put a glass of your sherry in it to give it an added taste.'

I use a story in my act which is based on fact. I once spent a week in a Blackpool boarding house in the days when I played the local clubs in the area. The woman who ran the place confronted me with this welcoming list of instructions:

'You'll find this place is home from home as long as you do what you're told. Don't use my immersion heater unless I tell you to, don't wear shoes on my fitted carpets and don't go in the other bedrooms. Don't bring girls back and don't touch my television set; I will select the programmes, I've paid cash for it and I don't want you messing about with it. Don't help yourself to food in the kitchen and don't bring fish and chips home with you, I can't stand the smell of them, and don't try frying up things for yourself either. I have six bedrooms and an L-shaped lounge and a room where you can write letters if you wish, and I have two bathrooms and two toilets, one upstairs and one down, but I'm warning you now, we don't use the toilet upstairs for solids.'

Solids! I'd heard of 'Number Twos' but this was ridiculous. I said to her one night: 'Have you been taking people in for a long time?' She sniffed and replied: 'Only since my husband passed away. All the neighbours sneered at our marriage because of the age difference. After all my husband was ninety-three and I'm just pushing forty.' (Which came as a bit of a shock – I thought she was dragging it.) She went on: 'Despite his advanced years, he was very agile ... I used to give him a blanket bath, rub him down with Fiery Jack and he was as good as new. Physically, our union was blessed; he was you know, capable. I didn't go short of anything. Mind you, I had to put him in a leather harness on the end of a pulley wheel, and if the back bedroom window was open he used to swing like hell, and once I had to get a sniper from Bisley to drop him down. We made love every Sunday morning in time with the gentle chimes of the church clock, until that terrible morning when it happened.' I said to her: 'Why, what happened?' She blew her nose and answered: 'A bloody fire engine went past.'

The Blackpool landlady held a lot of power in those days as far as show business was concerned. Before a summer production opened, the theatres held what was commonly known as a 'Landladies' Evening'. On that night, for free of course, the boarding-house owners came to see the show, and if they didn't like what they saw, then, my friend, you were finished. Some holidaymakers used to book in at a boarding house and, at the same time, ask the landlady to choose them a show and make the booking. Now you can see why they were so important.

At the end of the summer, the ladies migrated to Spain for the winter and Blackpool slid into hibernation. For me, at

any rate, Blackpool was at its best in the off-season. You could walk along the prom and allow the stark sea breezes to pummel your countenance into a ruddy mask and the highly charged ozone in the air filled the lungs with renewed vigour.

Habits have changed over the years and the Blackpool landlady is no longer enjoying the role that she once held. People started going abroad for vacations and once they saw what Spain and France had to offer, the old ways were not acceptable anymore. As one grizzled veteran, with over thirty years' experience of keeping a boarding house, said: 'They want too much today for the money they spend – not like before the war when folk were prepared to rough it. The buggers are spoilt rotten!'

But I mourn the passing of some of the little boarding houses. They had character, and for what you paid you got a just return. Many friendships were forged in the adversity of a guest house, and a lot of the landladies became almost part of the family as the summers rolled by.

Sometimes when I'm staying in a large hotel, I somehow yearn for that familiar strident voice trumpeting up the stairs: 'Come on, get theeself out, I want to do some Hoovering.'

A FINAL SALUTE

Some nights, when my beloved wife is away at one of her Luftwaffe reunions, and the children are out baiting pensioners, I often sit on the verandah with my karate-proficient, nymphomaniac Sudanese governess, and there muse about my life and times as a Lancashire-bred man. I will sit for hours, sipping my mint julep as the governess massages my thighs with pre-heated Algerian musk oil; I try to ignore the sound of the wife's mother wrestling with her Bullworker in the garage.

My Lancashire; memories of my youth. Scampering through the mean streets after the black maria as it took my dad away. I see my sweet mother on the roof of the church, her face a mask of strain as she pulled the lead off. Dear mother. It was from her that I got my love of music. As a child I would clamber onto her knee and whisper: 'Mummy, mummy, sing me a lullaby do.' She would smile serenely at me and say: 'Certainly my little cherub, my little bundle of joy, hold my beer whilst I fetch my banjo.'

Oh, how the years roll away. So many memories of times past. I see again the Holcombe Brook Frog Festival, an affair as old as the earth itself. During the ritual, comely maidens dressed in chest-length socks and cardboard hats leap over a duck that's been drugged in ointment, and men clad in only a bronze codpiece and blouse toss an iced manhole into a laced taxi. Thoughts like thistledown traversing back into scenic memoirs: the time I kissed Rosie Tunstall on the battlements of Croke Castle near Preston. Croke Castle, where Lady Rowena is said to have hidden Cromwell's teeth in a parcel of suet. Croke Castle, where King Charles contracted rabies from a Jewish orphan who pickled fruit.

Where are you now, Rosie? Oh, how I loved that winsome lass. That thick black hair down her back;

if only she'd had some on her head.

The majestic sweep of the Lancashire coast pervades the memory with its haunting beauty, and I hear once more the cry of the Fleetwood Swallow-backed Gull which lays eggs three times its own size. It's a funny sort of cry, it goes something like: 'AAAAAHHHHOOOWWOOW!'

My Lancashire. The bustle and energy of Liverpool, the great ships lying like predators in their berths; the white horses atop the surface of the Mersey; the sight of ragged children playing the age-old Liverpool game, 'Puss in the Corner'. In this childish pastime, one youngster lies in a corner and the others kick him in the puss.

Manchester, and its scurrying hordes of dedicated businessmen. There is no unemployment in Manchester, it's just an ugly rumour by a lot of people out of work. My father was a shift worker: if you ever mentioned work, he'd shift. Nobody is accusing him of being lazy, but he once fell asleep running for a bus.

The gentle hills above Bolton demand attention: soft sunlight dapples the pastures and blushes appear on the blackened stone walls that are a reminder of the feudal system. I remember there used to be so many cows grazing on those meadows that if you dropped your cap, you had to try on about six before you found the right one. Even to this very day, they still ask strangers this riddle: 'What's brown and sounds like a bell? ' Answer: 'Dung.'

Tales Of Old Lancashire I fondly recall the nights spent in the cosy inns around Great Eccleston in my courting days, when the future yawned before us and the wife was smaller than me. We'd hold hands; we always did, if we had ever let go we'd have killed one another. Gnarled old men would sit on the rough pub benches and recount many a lively tale of Old Lancashire. They told of Owd 'Arry, who was so mean, he once took the pendulum off a grandfather clock in case its shadow wore a hole in the wallpaper. He came home one night and found his wife with her head in the gas oven, so he said to his son: 'Put the kettle on before the shilling runs out.'

They spoke in awed tones of a man who had a dog that could do anything. In the morning, the dog would take a pan out of a cupboard, fill it with water and put an egg in it. After three minutes, the dog would take the egg out and place it on a tray with

some toast. It made the tea and then it would take the meal up to its master. An eye-witness told how he watched the dog put the tray on the bed, and then it cracked the top of the egg open for its master. Having done that, the dog then stood on its head with its legs apart. The eye-witness said: 'What does it do that for?' The dog's master said: 'I haven't got an egg cup.'

My Lancashire.

Old Josh from Little Lever knew everything. He had an incredibly retentive memory. For instance, did you know that if you inject a carrot with influenza it will attack a lavatory? Old Josh did. He was so wise in so many ways, and I revered him. When asked if the emergent Third World was a transmogrification into ethnic sublimation of cultural heritage, he replied: 'If a boiled owl's kneecap is left out to dry and the bag is full of cotton hats, it doesn't follow that earache is longer than a turnip root.' A simple truism from a country sage.

I have travelled far and wide in the world, but I always return to my beloved Lancashire. I have to really, I've only one change of underpants. I could live nowhere else, of this I swear. I have a home – how does the song go?

'Give me a home, where the buffalo roam
And I'll show you a house full of muck.'

Yes, I have a home, and the wife and I are happy on the whole; that's  what we live in, a hole. We've had our upsets: our cat gave birth in a bowler hat and the kittens grew up round-shouldered; but that's life. My mother-in-law is no trouble at all despite the things I have said about her. She sleeps all day in a box, and goes out at night. I've no idea what she does when she's out, but she has some pale friends.

I cannot imagine not being a Lancastrian. My children are trained in the ways of Lancashire and are wonderfully responsive to a rhino whip.

We never go abroad for holidays, every year we toddle off to one of Lancashire's better resorts:

Miresea-on-Crouch. I cannot recommend Miresea enough. You can walk for miles along the edge of the lime pits and the view from the fish manure works is breathtaking. There's so much to do there: you can try on gloves in a shop or listen to a Dutch clairvoyant giving lectures on amputation. Miresea by night is as romantic as Naples. On the jetty there is a Polish flute band which plays laments about the days of The Black Death, and the disused leper colony is ideal for kids wanting to play hide-and-seek.

Lighthouse Covers My money, what's left of it, is invested in Lancashire's future. In Rawtenstall there is a small company that makes lighthouse covers. It's a simple idea, really, but the covers keep the rain off them when they're not busy; I have shares in that firm. The main trouble is finding ladders long enough for the men to climb up so they can slide the covers over the lighthouse, but that's a problem that will soon be mastered.

We in Lancashire lead the world in ideas, and I am supremely confident that I can still get an overdraft.

It is perhaps fitting that the final salute should belong to Catchpole Worsley, the noted Lancashire poet and historian, who enriched the literary world with his observations of Northern life. Some of his sayings have been immortalized:

'A stitch in time will never make you trump.'
'When one door shuts, another bugger shuts.'
'If at first you don't succeed, cheat.'

He was a man for all seasons, and to me he epitomizes Lancashire. His parents were poor but poverty-stricken people and he was brought up in a house that was so small, when he turned the light off he was in bed before it was dark. He only had one change of nappy and, after six months, horses used to follow him with a bucket. His father loved him so much that when he was kidnapped by gypsies, his father drove the caravan for them.

At school he was the teacher's pet; she kept him in a cage. He was at sea when the *Titanic* went down; he was all right because he was travelling by iceberg at the time. He fell in love with a woman who had been married so many times, she had notches on her knickers. They were wed and there was trouble right from the start; in fact they had separate wedding cakes. They had three children, one of each, and when a chap came round to the house saying that he was collecting for the orphanage, Catchpole

immediately gave the fellow his kids.

His poetry is simple and direct, but tinged with sadness and bad spelling. He's dead now, of course; he went quite mad and began to think he was a Cornish pasty – then he flaked to death. Worsley *was* Lancashire, and I feel privileged to have been born in the same county. Lancashire, I salute you, queen of all the shires, and I leave you with this most pungent of Worsley's sayings:

'If all around you lose their heads
Then you'll be taller.'
It says it all.

Lightning Source UK Ltd.
Milton Keynes UK
UKOW012256100713

213506UK00001B/4/P